WALKING
THE TOPS

WALKING THE TOPS

Mountain Treks in Britain

Rex Bellamy

DAVID & CHARLES
Newton Abbot   London   North Pomfret (Vt)

British Library Cataloguing in Publication Data

Bellamy, Rex
Walking the tops.
1. Walking—Great Britain
I. Title
796.5'22   GV199.44.G7

ISBN 0-7153-8419-8

Typeset in Baskerville 11/12pt by
Typesetters (Birmingham) Ltd,
and printed in Great Britain
by Redwood Burn Ltd, Trowbridge, Wilts
for David & Charles (Publishers) Limited
Brunel House   Newton Abbot   Devon

Published in the United States of America
by David & Charles Inc
North Pomfret   Vermont 05053   USA

Contents

Introduction

These essays, self-contained yet sharing a common theme, describe one man's experiences and impressions while walking the tops from Dartmoor to Sutherland. The fifteen selected routes covered more than 180 miles as measured on the map, plus goodness knows how many more in ups and downs. The selection of areas and itineraries had to be somewhat arbitrary: but the former included all the high places of mainland Britain most familiar to hill-walkers, and the latter were designed to give author and readers an authentic taste of twelve distinctive, widely scattered chunks of mountainous terrain. The essays are arranged in sequence from south to north and could form the basis of a continuous tour of highland Britain. But they will be of more obvious benefit in introducing you, as they introduced me, to unfamiliar pleasures and challenges. We all have special affections for this or that stretch of long-familiar wilderness, but the range of such affections can be widened without being weakened. Life would hardly be worth the living unless some new horizon was beckoning. It is my hope, too, that these essays will recapture for you – as the writing of them did for me – the thrill of walking the tops, the fickle moods yet constant grandeur of the mountains, and the warmth of companionship we enjoy on the way.

It would be foolishly presumptuous to pretend that I know as much about these twelve areas as the specialists who have written so widely and so well about all of them. Nor is this a walkers' guidebook in the formal sense. I merely went out to Britain's high places to see what they had to say to me and then gathered the fruits of that subjective research into a coherent form. The idea was to assimilate the flavour of all the components so that they could be appreciated separately, and also as a whole. I make no apologies for taking an interest in local history, for savouring the joys of food and wine and good company, for waxing romantic about the good times and gloomy about the bad, or for the deficiencies arising from idleness or indiscretion. I wandered off course occasionally, but there is an old saying among hill-walkers that the man who never got lost never got very far. This book tells you exactly how it was: what occurred, and how I felt about it. If you should feel that we are walking shoulder to shoulder – gazing at the same distant splendours (or peering through the same fog), crunching over the same rock and heather, and making the same mistakes – then *Walking the Tops* is succeeding in its purpose.

I have tried to be original as well as honest. The easy way to write such a book would be to sit in a library and borrow freely from the experience and expertise of others. To some extent I had to do that, because basic research was essential. But then I went out and got my boots mucky. There is nothing second-hand about the walks described here. They happened – and because they happened and I have told you the truth about them, there is much in this book that will ring bells in the minds of all hill-walkers. Such a book is one man's work but every man's memories. There is nothing exclusive about the empty loneliness of high places, the sighing of the wind, the trickle of infant streams, and the sound of boots on bogs or boulders.

Most of the walks amounted to much more than afternoon strolls, but only on the Glyders – and, briefly, Ingleborough – were conditions sufficiently bad to exceed the normal limits of a hill-walker's competence. Do not be disheartened by the references to fog and rain, ice and snow. Circumstances forced me to undertake all these excursions – except for those in Scotland – between September and March. You will probably be luckier in

8

your timing and weather. Moreover, I am in my middle fifties. Most of you will be younger and therefore more energetic and ambitious. You may seek tougher challenges. But remember that scrambling about on mountains can be perilous. Like the countryside as a whole, mountains are best appreciated if we know them in all seasons and all moods, but they are subject to sudden climatic changes. Fog is a persistent hazard, and the temperature drops rapidly as height is gained. An altitude harmless enough in the Alps can be dangerous in Britain. We have very few tops that reach 4,000ft (about 1,219m), but conditions at half that height can be bad enough to kill.

These walks are primarily for those who already have a basic knowledge of hill-craft. They are not suitable for the very young, the very old, or the infirm. Nor, on the other hand, are they severe enough to tempt the 'tigers' of the mountaineering school. They are for that vast majority in between: the hill-walkers, the ramblers who like to roam on the tops, the men and women who enjoy a strenuous day out that may last for up to ten hours. All the itineraries – those I actually did and the suggested alternatives at the end of every chapter – presuppose that readers know how to use an Ordnance Survey map (readily available at public libraries these days) and, when necessary, a compass. At the same time I have assembled a great deal of information and advice that will be useful to the inexperienced. The usual practice is to condense this into the introduction, or into a single chapter, but that seems to me rather indigestible. Instead, this or that aspect of hill-craft is discussed as we go along, whenever it is appropriate. Everything important crops up sooner or later, and the index will direct you to guidance on any particular subject.

High places can teach us a great deal, and not merely about hill-craft. Days on the mountains can be enriched by a wide range of relevant interests: perhaps geography, geology, or meteorology; perhaps flora and fauna, fungi,

entomology (insects), or ornithology (birds); perhaps
photography; or history and prehistory. All over highland
Britain there is evidence of primitive communities and
the crude farming and mining that preceded the machine
age and the Industrial Revolution. Within a few thousand
years the highland forests were cleared, the soils
deteriorated, moorland and bogs developed, and the
population shifted downwards. Crop cultivation gave way
to stock raising, and stock raising gave way to sheep.
There is not much indication of those ancient highland
communities now: perhaps some tell-tale ridges in a field,
the softened outline of earthworks, a heap of overgrown
rubble, a quaint place-name. But walk carefully on the
hills. You walk among ghosts.

Transhumance, the seasonal shifting of cattle between
highland and lowland pastures, became pointless when
the upper grazing areas declined into the striking but,
from a farming point of view, useless wilderness we know
today. But the hills still provide an income for farmers
and highland estates. So we have to close gates, avoid
damage to fences, walls, and hedges, and keep to the
paths when crossing farmland. We have to keep dogs
under control and take care not to disturb livestock or
wildlife. Litter is inexcusable, because it spoils the scenery
for others and can cause injury or illness to any birds or
beasts who happen to tread on it or eat it. In short, we
simply have to behave with the common sense and
courtesy we expect from others.

All this is easier to remember if we take our time. In the
mountains, haste is bad practice anyway, partly because
it leaves no time to stand and stare and partly because it
will probably cause distress. Leaders must set a pace that
can be comfortably and consistently maintained by the
slowest member of the party. At the same time, rhythm is
important – and rhythm is broken by stops that are too
frequent or too prolonged. The best hill-walkers never
hurry but seldom stop, except to admire the view,
exchange a few words with other ramblers, take a photo-

graph, or allow children or dogs to enjoy some adventure. One should be motionless for no more than five minutes an hour unless lunching, which inevitably breaks the rhythm.

There are pretty walks in valleys and dramatic walks over passes, but it is on the tops, with nothing pressing in on us, that the spirit has most room to expand. It is on the tops that we have to grapple most strenuously with the exhilarating challenges of our natural environment – and take the measure of our strengths and weaknesses. It is on the tops that we can let loose the adventurer and the poet lurking restlessly within all of us. And it is on the tops, walking through clouds and silence, that we can most easily come to terms with yesterday and tomorrow. Along the way, we can listen to the music of birds and brooks, smell the flowers and the moors, and share the laughter of friends.

I have written a book about all that.

Rex Bellamy
Bilberry Cottage, Seale

1

A Police Escort on Dartmoor

◆

Dartmoor is unique in its compact diversity, in its stimulating assortment of topographic samples and social history. There are days – far more of them than Dartmoor's reputation suggests – when the barren wilderness can, in its own way, be almost as charming as the flanking valleys. And the moors are always a challenge, partly because of their desolate nature and partly because Dartmoor's fickle climate can make the place horribly wet and cold and foggy and lonely. The tops are evidently hills rather than mountains, though High Willhays (2,038ft or 621m) and its neighbour Yes Tor (2,030ft or 619m) both qualify, by British standards, for mountainous status: ie, both exceed 2,000ft (610m) and have summits enclosed, on the map, by single, unbroken contour lines.

Granted this qualification, plus the fact that they command impressive views on a clear day, High Willhays and Yes Tor nevertheless lack the character of mountains. There is nothing striking about them, they are easily accessible via rough roads, and both lie within one of Dartmoor's three artillery ranges (to avoid perforating possibilities, always check firing days at the post office before legging it across Dartmoor). In terms of temptation, High Willhays and Yes Tor cannot be prominently ranked among British tops. But the hill-walker should be wary of regarding them as the stars of the show. The supporting cast twinkles far more brightly. And the overall effect can be enchanting.

Dartmoor certainly has an aura of mystery about it,

but mystery and beauty are perfectly compatible. Indeed, each enhances the other. Dartmoor's sombre associations are based on its prison and the exaggerated half-truths of legend. I had nibbled at its fringes, driven across it, read about it, heard about it: and did not regard the place as an urgent priority for a hill-walker. There was this mental image of a gloomy, lumpy, soggy wasteland, its visual monotony relieved only by granite tors – promoted to isolated prominence because their former wrappings had been reduced in stature by centuries of erosive weathering. Yes, I knew about the remnants of pre-historic settlements, primitive farming and mining, the prison, the wild ponies, the fictional Hound of the Baskervilles, and the military training areas – at once hazardous and, in their effect on the landscape, somewhat taming. But all that was the small change of knowledge. Essentially I went to Dartmoor with an open, uncluttered mind and a suspicion that the trip might be more of a chore than a pleasure. There was more spectacular hill-walking to be done elsewhere: and scenery just as pretty as that to be found where infant rivers tumble from the moors into the wooded valleys ('cleaves') of Dartmoor's lush periphery. The flaw in such armchair preconceptions is that, though their general tendency may be sound, a rudimentary acquaintance with components gives us no more than a hint of the character of the whole. We may study the chef's shopping list but be totally wrong in predicting the quality of the dinner. In short, I was only half-right about Dartmoor.

Luckily I was granted good companions who knew their stuff: the police. The brooding presence of that famous old prison was coincidental. An extra-mural police escort was sound insurance anyway, because they knew their way about Dartmoor and I did not. To reverse a cliché, they could help me with my enquiries. So I followed up a suggestion that the Metropolitan Police Cadet School might tolerate a middle-aged super-numerary during their preparations for the annual 10

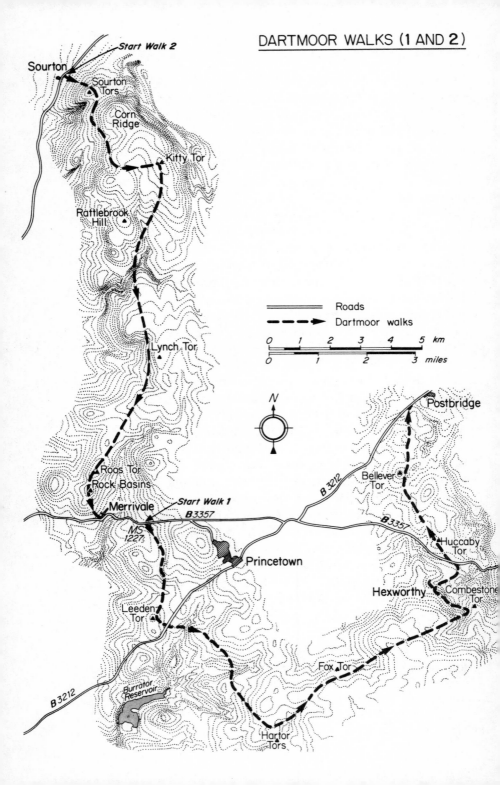

Tors Expedition. Tony Cunningham, who was in charge of adventure training, and Ron Skinner, the physical education director, boldly agreed to take a chance. For all they knew, I might have only one good leg and be equally unstable between the ears – and any such misgivings were presumably even more prevalent among the staff and cadets who would be lumbered with me on Dartmoor. Whatever their reservations, they put me in protective custody.

Leaving the A30 at Whiddon Down (more of Whiddon in a moment), I plunged into those sunken, twisting, roller-coaster lanes dominated by the gently swelling dome of Dartmoor's mostly bare uplands. Before examining the topography in more tiring detail I reserved remedial comforts at the Three Crowns in the outrageously photogenic market town of Chagford, which seemed to be posing in readiness for the camera. A film crew, in fact, were in residence at the Three Crowns. Every day, they breakfasted early before trundling out to Beardown Tors, with the Royal Marines among them, to reconstruct episodes from the Falklands conflict. The Marines, it transpired, were equally versatile as bar-room entertainers. Chagford ('chag' is dialect for gorse) has the air of casual neatness that usually indicates self-confident prosperity. It was one of the original stannary towns – from the Latin 'stannum', for tin – at which miners had their tin weighed and taxed. The industry was governed by the miners' stannary courts, which had a status hovering between that of a powerful trade union and a local parliament. These courts were not formally abolished until 1897 but the way of life they represented had begun to slip back into history with the sixteenth century. Chagford has long since assumed a similarly influential role as a tourists' centre handy for Dartmoor to the west and, to the east, the wooded ravine of the Teign.

The granite-built Three Crowns, opposite the churchyard near the town's attractive little square, is a rambling old place with idiosyncratic leanings – exemplified, in my room, by a mirror and a bedside table. That table's compromise with the horizontal was so uneasy that loose change slid gently onto the carpet. Such disorientating tilts should not, I noted, be confused with the effects of any forthcoming excess of exercise or draught cider. The Three Crowns was built as a manor house for a sixteenth-century Chagford celebrity, Sir John Whiddon, who could be engagingly quirky in his disregard for some of the traditional customs of the judiciary. He was the first judge to ride to Westminster Hall on a horse rather than a mule, and legend has it that at a time of civil unrest he once sat on the bench in full armour except, presumably, for doffing his helmet. The family had strong roots in Chagford. In 1641 Mary Whiddon was accidentally shot and killed by a jealous suitor at the altar of Chagford Church. That incident achieved fictional embellishment and enduring renown when R. D. Blackmore shifted it about forty miles and as many years, to Oare, where Carver Doone shot Lorna as she was standing at the altar with John Ridd. The author was an Exmoor man and much of the novel has historic parallels. Two years after Mary Whiddon's death Chagford was the scene of another prematurely terminal drama. This time its victim was a sensitive, remarkably talented young Cornishman, Sidney Godolphin, who became MP for Helston at the age of eighteen and also attained distinction as a poet. During the Civil War he mustered a royalist force in Cornwall and added its weight to an army advancing into Devon. Shot in a leg during a skirmish with parliamentary troops at Chagford, Godolphin fell from his horse and, bleeding heavily, was carried to a stone seat in the porch of what is now the Three Crowns. There he died.

As arranged, I reported to the police, who revived the jaded traveller with tea before discussing the morrow. They were staying at a youth hostel in the charming hamlet of Gidleigh, a natural bird sanctuary perched at 900ft (275m) on the edge of the moor. The place has medieval remnants and, as if arrested in time, its lay-out is still much as it was in the fourteenth century. In such a context the police presence (six staff and twenty cadets) seemed excessive. Come to that, even one bobby on a bicycle would have seemed excessive. But the 10 Tors Expedition is one of the sparks that fires the adventure-training programme and nothing is left to chance in preparing for it. More than two months before the event the lads were enduring a series of sharpening tests before teams of six were chosen from short lists of ten. The Expedition's awards system demands cross-Dartmoor walking against the clock, between 7am on Saturday and 5pm on Sunday, with an overnight camp. The mileage (maximum 55) varies according to the age category. The competitors are teenagers from the armed services, the police, and a variety of youth organisations. There are classes for girls and even the disabled – in wheelchairs, with pushers. Officially the Expedition is non-competitive but teams are inevitably keen to return faster times than their rivals. There are local reservations, even some resentment, about the actual and potential inconvenience of this mass assault on Dartmoor. And Alan Mattingly, secretary of the Ramblers' Association, says that although they welcome initiatives that encourage youngsters to walk the hills, they are not particularly happy with the way the Expedition is run – 'the razzamatazz, the noise, the helicopters, the Army vehicles' – and would like it to be more informal. That is my own gut reaction. At the same time it must be admitted that young, inexperienced ramblers would cause less anxiety to themselves and others if all had the advantage – as, for example, the police cadets have – of expert, disciplined training in hill-craft.

All that mattered, strictly, was that Mick Yeates would collect me from the Three Crowns next morning and deliver me to the mercies of ten cadets, aged sixteen to eighteen, who would then demonstrate their capacity to walk fast for 17 map miles (ignoring undulations) with no more than brief breathers. It was only slightly reassuring that Mick – together with George Pether, the cadets' Expedition manager, and Eric Stroud, the civilian driver – would twice intercept us en route to make a quick body count from their Land Rover. With no wish to add to their doubts about the unknown quantity in their midst, I withheld some relevant information: during the four preceding days I had lurched feverishly about the house with some throat and chest virus that was doing my breathing apparatus no good at all. Forget it. Roy Emerson, a great tennis player and exemplary sportsman, used to say that if you were not fit you did not go on court. If you went on court, you were fit. Whatever happened, no excuses. And I was on court. I was fortunate, too: because until the end of the day our deviations from the horizontal were to make only benign demands on ailing lungs.

Come morning, Mick Yeates arrived in the Land Rover and we drove across the moor past the lonely Warren House Inn and, more distantly, Wistman's Wood and Princetown. The inn was a welcome refuge for travellers in the days when tourists ('grockles') were rare and Dartmoor was more of a wilderness than it is now. Local tin miners were regular clients. The inn's name and its three-rabbit sign are reminders that for centuries rabbits were bred in Headland Warren, across the road, and sold for their meat and skins. Wistman's Wood is one of nature's jokes: gnarled dwarf oaks, older than even oaks should be (their clock stopped), growing at 1,350ft (411m) amid the boulder rubble locally known as 'clitter'. This is no place for trees, however eccentric. Clitter is a feature of Dartmoor's many tors and the word 'tor', a variant of 'tower' or 'heap', is more prevalent on Dartmoor than anywhere else. The settlement of Princetown was founded in 1785 to house the work-force of Sir Thomas Tyrwhitt. He was private secretary to George III's eldest son, the Prince of Wales, and leased a chunk of Dartmoor from the Duchy of Cornwall. Sir Thomas was enterprising. He grew flax, quarried

18

granite, and installed a primitive railway and canal. Bleakly exposed at 1,400ft (427m), Princetown lacked the charm to attract all the labourers he needed. Sir Thomas reinforced them by building a prison to accommodate French captives from the Napoleonic wars, who had previously been packed into prison ships at Plymouth. The prison was finished in 1809 and the French inmates were later replaced by Americans captured during the war of 1812–14. After that there was no use for the place until 1850, when it was renovated and given its familiar role as a prison for long-term convicts.

We pulled in at a walled parking area alongside the B3357, just short of Merrivale. George and Eric turned up with the cadets and then left, with Mick, to warn the local police of our planned route: that essential precaution for all hill-walkers in remote country. Ten teenagers and an appendage set off almost due south at a brisk pace. Across mossy, springy grass, a rough track by disused quarries, and the course of that old railway. The morning was sunny, distantly grey, and a skylark was singing us on our way. Did I say 'brisk pace'? It was a cracker. At Leeden Tor (1,277ft or 389m) the team leader, Brad, turned to his charges. 'Keep this up,' he said, 'and we'll be back before we started.' Team leaders need to know about psychology. The Land Rover was waiting as we crossed the B3212. The 'staff' were making sure there were still eleven vertical bodies. George got out and gave me a questioning look lightly flavoured with amused compassion. We hardly broke stride in exchanging greetings. A passing pantechnicon was emblazoned with the words 'National Blood Transfusion Service'. I was in a mood to notice things like that. Still, all I had to do was leg-work. The team leader and navigator were doing the head-work. These cadets are well organised.

Our route now veered south-east. First past the visual oddity of an aqueduct in which the water was driven gently upwards by the force of a tumbling stream. Then up to the moorland of ridges and tors with, away to the west, Burrator Reservoir – Plymouth's main water supply – and its encasing woodland. To the east was one of the stone crosses, hewn from single blocks of granite, in which Dartmoor abounds. Often erected on tracks linking monasteries, they served as guides to travellers and sometimes marked medieval boundaries. Beyond Down Tor (1,201ft or 366m) we bisected a stone row stretching across the bare upland from a stone circle. Here, too, were hut circles, remnants of the wigwam-shaped dwellings of Dartmoor's prehistoric population. The best surviving example of these settlements is Grimspound, about two miles east of the Warren House Inn. In those days the climate was drier and today's peat was still woodland. But the climate worsened and, in time, the people and the natural woodland vanished from the face of Dartmoor. The landscape had changed by the time medieval farmers and miners moved in. Now Dartmoor has the accentuated loneliness peculiar to a crowd of ghosts.

We were not hanging about, anyway. We sped on across a mostly trackless expanse of heather and rock. Past groups of the wild ponies (unexpectedly variegated in their colouring) whose ancestors were often used as packhorses. Past hefty, hornless Galloways with shaggy black coats. Past the inevitable sheep. There was no sound except for the skylarks, the clump of boots, and the swish of rainproof legwear. Crossing a cart track and a wall, we paused by Hartor Tors. Two hours and five minutes, so far, with no time to stand and stare. There were kind enquiries about how the pace was affecting me. It was, I confessed, hotter than my usual pace but no more than I had expected. With luck I would survive. 'Good,' said Brad, 'because we haven't brought a stretcher.'

We swung round to the north-east, towards Dartmoor at its dodgiest – and as we did so the fair morning gave way to fog. Conscious that bog plus fog adds up to nothing but bad news (except for the most artless of

20

versifiers), Brad arranged us in a compact arrowhead formation to deter the absent-minded from straying into the adjacent 'Dartmoor Stables', in which many a wild pony has been wetly interred. Dartmoor's most infamous hazard has often been exaggerated for dramatic effect. But bogs are at best unpleasant and at worst lethal. They come in several varieties. The hill-walker must fasten in his mind two basic facts: the bright green carpet of moss known as sphagnum marks a no-go area and the 'quaker' or 'featherbed' must be avoided at all costs. Sphagnum looks attractive and has its uses: as a packing material for horticulturists, as a mild antibiotic, and even (it is said) as a source of improvised nappies for the babies of Lapland. What matters to you and me is that, sponge-like, it has large cells which can absorb large quantities of water and, even more important, it is rootless. In other words, sphagnum gives a false impression of stability. Which brings us to the perils of the 'quaker' or 'featherbed' or, more formally, the quagmire. This can be a killer because it consists of a crater filled with watery, oozy nastiness disguised beneath a shaky layer of rotten vegetation and sphagnum that may, or may not, support one's weight.

Such cautionary thoughts sprang easily to mind in the fog because, at the time, we were close to the renowned 'quaker' known as Foxtor Mires. This, supposedly, was the 'Grimpen Mire' ('a false step yonder means death to man or beast') where Sherlock Holmes emptied five barrels of his revolver into the Hound of the Baskervilles. Closer and even more ghoulish in its legendary associations was Childe's Tomb on the flank of Fox Tor. 'Childe' was formerly an honourable title, like the Spanish 'infante', applied to a youth of noble birth. The story goes that Childe the Hunter, a considerable landowner at Plymstock (Plymouth), was caught in a blizzard on Dartmoor and tried to ride it out. He failed, and became desperate in his need for shelter and warmth. Displaying a horribly callous sense of initiative, he killed his horse, cut it open, emptied the contents, and curled up inside. But it did him no good. A cross marks the spot.

As usual, visibility improved as we began to lose height. South of Fox Tor we had a 35 minute lunch break. A hill-walker's appetite can be as unconventional as a pregnant woman's and, as is often the case, all I needed was fluids: hot soup and a sip of red wine. Exercise gives the body enough work to do, without the additional stress of absorbing solid food: but such compact and nourishing goodies as chocolate, fruit cake, and oranges are essential for the occasional, refuelling nibble. Alcohol must be treated with discretion because it can impair the judgement, especially when one is tired. I was interested, and impressed, by the way individual cadets carried items to satisfy communal needs. One even had a plastic dustbin liner so that the team's garbage would not be left lying about on Dartmoor. For this purpose I always shove a loaf-wrapper into a rucksack pocket. The weather had cleared and there were attractive views across the gentle, sunlit valley of the West Dart as we slogged across the moor. The afternoon shadows were lengthening. It was a joy to be out on such a day, though the relentless pace was tiring. George, Mick and Eric were waiting for us at Combestone Tor and during a 10 minute break I was briefly tempted by a hint that I could quit now if I wanted to. But no self-respecting sportsman, past or present, likes the idea of retiring hurt. Still batting down to number eleven, we followed the lane across a charming little bridge, swung past Hexworthy's well-known Forest Inn, and then paused for a moment at Huccaby Bridge, a lovely spot on the West Dart where otters sometimes gather at playtime. How apt it was, in such a setting, to find a church bearing the name of a painter, Raphael (St Raphael is also one of the patron saints of travellers).

Unfortunately the aesthetic senses were swiftly dulled by the ascent to the B3357 and, on the moor again, up to Huccaby Tor. I shall remember the name, because that last uphill stretch emptied my bottle. The combination of chest virus, pace, and the kind of terrain measured by clinometers now left me with very little to give. Mercifully the cadets occasionally stopped to check the route to and beyond Laughter Tor. We came to a path between two handsome conifer woods and veered right, into one of them, for the last downhill walk to Postbridge – and a car park containing George, Mick, Eric, a Land Rover and the cadets' coach. It was a beautiful evening, all birdsong and soft shadows. The 17 miles had taken 6 hours and 55 minutes. Subtract the 55 minutes, the cumulative time for breaks, and we had walked for 6 hours. The cadets were pleased because they were an hour inside *their* schedule, which meant that the middle-aged supernumerary felt slightly smug. For a moment, anyway. Then I sat down abruptly on the steps of the coach as the agony of cramp knotted the calf muscles of one leg. Mick, who knows about things like that, sorted it out in no time. But I resisted the temptation to stroll across the road for a detailed examination of Dartmoor's most impressive clapper bridge. These consist of unworked granite slabs supported by granite piers. Crude and sturdy, they date from the Middle Ages (like the crosses) and were essential features of the packhorse tracks that preceded roads.

To save his blushes I will not name the hardy adventure-training specialist who, having driven me back to the Three Crowns, bravely stood at the bar drinking a Pimm's: an ornate, brandy-based concoction trimmed with fruit and veg. I misheard his preference, put it down to eccentricity, and happened to order the drinks while he was out of the room. Confronted by the kind of refreshment ladies order, so that they can simultaneously eat and drink and have something to play with, that embarrassed model of virility displayed the savoir-faire of a diplomat. First he undressed the Pimm's and drank it. Then he ordered another round – and got the Pils he wanted.

Shortly afterwards, while lying in a hot bath at rather less than arm's length from a second pint of draught cider, I reflected on the day. In hill-walking as in competitive sport, there are two obvious ways of exhausting a man: by maintaining a hot pace or by breaking his rhythm. Examples from tennis are Connors on the one hand and McEnroe on the other. Examples from hill-walking are 'cadets' pace' and rock work – the latter because, on rocky ground, the repeated vertical and lateral adjustments are far more tiring than a consistent stride. Still musing on such great truths, I returned to the bar for a rendezvous with the police: not merely George, Mick and Eric, but also Tim Potts, Derek Fanning (I was to meet them later in North Wales) and Les Gibbons, who had spent the day in tripartite surveillance of the older cadets. The company included the Royal Marines and a genially extrovert country-and-western singer, self-styled 'Sticks the Bandit', who quickly realised that he had accomplished allies. These three disparate segments of humanity – police, Marines, and ballad singer – swiftly found common cause in the individual and corporate pleasures of musical entertainment. George Pether ('I'm just a drummer') revealed an intimate acquaintance with the Rock Island Line, whatever that may be, and the rigours of heaving coal. Les Gibbons used his right arm to dramatic effect in declamatory renderings of patriotic songs. The Marines explored the rhythmic possibilities of spoons and trays and the sexual connotations of threshing machines. The landlord told stories, the landlady sang sweet Irish airs, 'Sticks' stitched all the pieces together, and the joy of that evening was non-stop. I have enjoyed many evenings of good fellowship among chance acquaintances, but none to match this in the versatile, sustained quality of its improvised entertainment. By bedtime, whenever that was, I was feeling no pain at all. Huccaby Tor was a memory mislaid.

The police, however, had not done with me yet. We just had time to fit in a half-day. This was an exhilarating walk and, for a 'tops' specialist, can be even more highly recommended than its predecessor. The weather was fine and clear and the sweeping views across Dartmoor were superb. Again, the pace was punishing but, this time, more so for the cadets than for me. From the church at Sourton, on the A386, we climbed about 650ft (200m) in half a mile to Sourton Tors (1,444ft or 440m) at a lung-searching tempo. But Mick Yeates had come with us in the role of drover. Initially packless, he heard the distressed breathing, took my rucksack, and carried it all the way to Merrivale in spite of half-hearted cavilling. Moreover, having whipped the cadets into a series of exhausting jogs beyond my capacity, he had little choice but to join me taking the second half of the course at a conversational pace while the boys raced ahead.

From Sourton Tors we swung round the western flank of Corn Ridge and up a peaty, heathery track to Kitty Tor (1,919ft or 585m). It was exactly an hour since we had given up the luxury of wheels. The rest of the route was almost due south. There was much trackless, hummocky bog-trotting as we passed east of Rattlebrook Hill (1,774ft or 541m) and Hare Tor (1,743ft or 531m) to a stony crossing of the young, musical Tavy: just a little upstream from the awful gorge of Tavy Cleave. It was at this point that Mick, feeling playful, urged the cadets across the always adjacent frontier between walking and jogging. In the process the field placings acquired a startled longstop. We reached Lynch Tor (1,696ft or 517m) after 2 hours and 20 minutes. The Land Rover was parked in a lane down to the west, and George and Eric drifted into view, ambling up to intersect our route. Just checking. The next two miles or so were the bonne bouche of the walk. The western flank of Dartmoor and its distant environs opened out before us as if someone had drawn back a curtain. That airy panorama was marvellous. We could see the ancient, simple little church perched on the volcanic rock of Brent Tor. To the south there was even a glimpse of Plymouth Sound. Motionless, as if posing, a horse and rider were etched on the eastern skyline. And before us, massed on open ground, was the colourful bustle of a hunt, with the urgent summons of hounds and horn echoing across the bare land. As Mick said, whatever one's opinions about foxhunting, it is certainly spectacular.

And it was somewhere hereabouts that, after Mick had turned away to urinate, a straight-faced cadet courteously enquired: 'Which way's the wind blowing, sir?'

On to Roos Tor and Rock Basins (1,493ft or 455m) and then down to Merrivale and a momentary sense of disappointment – because George, Eric and the cadets were waiting for us in the coach, rather than the Dartmoor Inn. We had covered about 11 map miles in 3¾ hours, finishing little more than half a mile from the previous day's starting point. George drove me back to Chagford for a farewell drink. The party was over. But in a day and a half I had lost 5lb and acquired an affectionate, respectful regard for Dartmoor and adventure training, police-style. True, I had been lucky in my companions and in the fact that Dartmoor had been on its best behaviour: firm going and windlessly dry, clear weather. Dartmoor's two dominant features had on this occasion been totally exposed for our pleasure and enlightenment: the wild, central dome of moorland and, tucked into its flanks, the wooded valleys with their grey villages and steeply banked, half-hidden lanes. As for the cadets, I wish all youngsters could similarly benefit from exercises encouraging physical and mental fitness, discipline, self-reliance and stickability. All that induces a sense of individual and corporate responsibility that helps them not only in their careers, but in the wider challenges of life as a whole. As Tim Potts put it, a two-way advantage of adventure training is that 'they can find out about themselves and we can find out about them'. Of all sports and recreations, there is none better than hill-walking (extended, if you like, to rock-climbing and mountaineering) to develop the character of the young and teach them the measure of their own strengths and weaknesses.

Other suggested walks

1 The two walks described could be combined in a long and tiring day, more than 28 miles, from Sourton to Postbridge. A shorter alternative would be to finish at Combestone Tor or Hexworthy.

2 Equally demanding is the north–south crossing from Belstone or Sticklepath to Bittaford, via Cawsand Hill, Wild Tor, Hangingstone Hill, Whitehorse Hill, the valley of the East Dart, Postbridge (a possible terminus), Bellever Forest, Huccaby Tor, Dartmeet, Combestone Tor, Ryder's Hill and Ugborough Moor.

3 A 'boomerang' walk, starting and finishing at Post-bridge, can take in Wistman's Wood, Lydford Tor, Cowsic River, Cut Hill, Black Hill, Cranmere Pool, East Dart Head, Sandy Hole Pass, and the Beehive Hut.

4 Meldon Dam, Longstone Hill, Black Tor, Fordsland Ledge, High Willhays, Yes Tor, and a choice of routes to Belstone or Okehampton: thus crossing highest Dartmoor.

2

Pen y Fan and the Paras

————◆————

Less than 30 miles, as the crow flies, spans the heights that stand almost shoulder to shoulder from the gently whalebacked, quadri-ridged Black Mountains in the east and over the Brecon Beacons to the Black Mountain in the west. Nothing quite reaches the magical figure of 3,000ft (914m) and the rock is not of a kind to tempt mountaineers. But this is a land that might have been created for the exclusive delectation of the hill-walker: beautiful, remote, challenging, but seldom intimidating. One could spend days browsing along the tops, with contemplative overnight pauses at well-chosen inns tucked away in the valleys. Start, perhaps, with Waun Fach and Pen y Gader-Fawr, and then head towards Carmarthen Bay via Pen y Fan, Fan Fawr, Fan Gihirych and Fan Brycheiniog. Only the insensitive could resist the many alluring diversions to this or that beckoning summit along the way. But a week would do it. Two would do it better.

The heart, of course, is the Brecon Beacons, so named because of their former use as obvious locations for signalling fires. Four valleys are scooped out of their northern flanks. The corniced faces, plunging almost 600ft (180m), look ridiculously like a much magnified version of those soaring, concave waves in the opening sequence of the American television series, 'Hawaii Five-O'. These are crumbling cliffs rather than sheer falls of solid rock, because the Beacons are the highest chunk of Old Red Sandstone in the British Isles. But there are a host of well-clothed access routes to a craggy escarpment. This swings from east to west in a succession of loops that might have been fashioned out of the Earth's

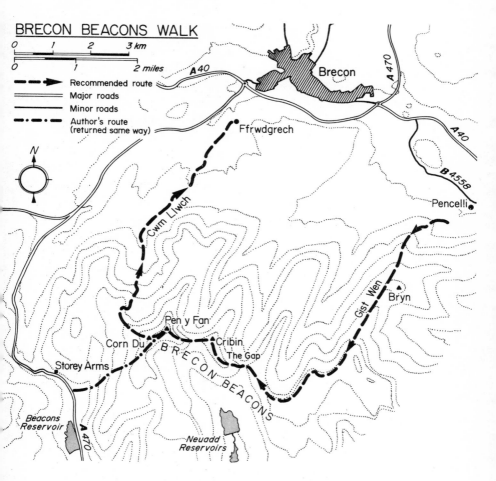

BRECON BEACONS WALK

0   1   2   3 km
0   1   2 miles

— —▶ Recommended route
═══   Major roads
──── Minor roads
—·—·— Author's route
        (returned same way)

A 40
Brecon
A 470
A 40
B 4558
Pencelli
Ffrwdgrech
N
Cwm Llwch
Gist Wen
Bryn
Pen y Fan
Corn Du
Cribin
The Gap
Storey Arms
BRECON BEACONS
Beacons
Reservoir
A 470
Neuadd
Reservoirs

crust by an unimaginably large pastry-cutter. The
northern approach is the most impressive.

A day on the hills, though, is a gamble with the
weather: and this time I lost. There had been warnings
enough. The Beacons were up there somewhere, but
there was no sign of them when I arrived late one misty
afternoon in March and called at the mountain centre, a
mile and a half off the A470 at Libanus. The elderly
custodian was amiably helpful but discouraging, even
pessimistic. I should have come a week earlier, he said.
The weather was unlikely to improve. He suggested that
the short, well-trodden tourist track might be the best

investment – that if I must go, the only reasonable thing to do was to get to the top and back again as quickly as possible. There was a hint that, if wise, I would forget the whole thing and go home. He confessed, however, that he did not much care for hill-walking anyway. Was it possible that prejudice was inducing him to overplay the role of Jeremiah? But next morning, in the national park office at Brecon, the head warden was reading the same script. Friendly and practical, he nevertheless scattered dampening words on the fire of my enthusiasm. It was hardly worth while going up, he said, because I wouldn't see anything. Waxing sardonic, he asked if I had a compass and added: 'You won't forget to leave a note on the car windscreen, in case we have to come looking for you?'

Brecon itself was somewhat deficient in the party spirit. The place was grey and dank and quiet, as if mourning the dead and expecting more imminently. Beautifully located, where the Honddu and Tarell flow into the Usk amid encircling hills, the town developed around an eleventh-century castle built for the local Norman conqueror, Bernard of Newmarch or, more correctly, Neufmarché, east of Rouen. He came to Britain with the original Conqueror and, finding a Norman lass who took his fancy, married her and settled in Herefordshire. It was much to his credit that he was among the Norman lords who rebelled against that nasty man, William Rufus. Later Bernard invaded the Brecon (or Brecknock) region, settled there, and had his castle built. The place was renovated in the reign of Edward I but destroyed during the Cromwell era. Its remnants were to be incorporated in the grounds of a hotel. Bernard, a busy builder, also founded and endowed Brecon's priory of St John and made it subordinate to the Benedictine abbey at Battle in Sussex. A permanent reminder of the connection is the little village of Battle, 3 miles north-west of Brecon. Bernard, in short, was a remarkable man who planted the seeds from which grew the Brecon we know today. The

Romans preceded him but their 'Bannium' – now Caer Bannau or Y Gaer – was south of Battle by the confluence of the Yscir and the Usk. Give or take a year or two, their settlement was founded in AD 75, rebuilt in 105, and abandoned in 140. Much of the masonry was used to build Bernard's castle.

An ancient British tribe, the Silures, gave the Romans some disconcerting lessons in primitive guerilla warfare. Their name was revived by its application to a distinguished poet, Henry Vaughan (1622–95). He was known as the 'Silurist' because he was born a few miles down the Usk at Newton (Llansantffraed), worked in Brecon as a doctor for five years, and always had a great affection for the area. Even better known, because she was in the entertainment business, was the actress and occasional model, Sarah Siddons (1755–1831), who was born in Brecon at a public house called the Shoulder of Mutton. Hot stuff in such roles as Lady Macbeth, Ophelia, and Desdemona, she belonged to the declamatory school and may have been the finest of all British tragediennes. Her brother Charles Kemble (1775–1854), also born at Brecon, was well known in Shakespearean supporting roles. They were among the twelve children of the actor–manager Roger Kemble and his wife Sarah, who decided to turn the family into a travelling dramatic company. They could hardly help it. Which reminds me that Rachel (Elisa Felix), the famous French tragedienne of the same era, was once asked why she had so many lovers but never married. 'I don't mind tenants,' she said, 'but I won't have owners.' This philosophy differed sharply from that of another Brecon celebrity, Adelina Patti (1843–1919), who married three times – ultimately at the Roman Catholic church in Glamorgan Street. Born in Madrid of Italian parents, the renowned coloratura soprano had an unusually long career, from 1860 until her farewell concert in 1906. One of her most popular encores was 'Home, sweet home', which no longer seems the most obvious of encores for an opera singer. In those

31

days it was, because the song had its first airing in a
Covent Garden opera twenty years before Madame Patti
was born. In her case, home was a castle at Craig-y-Nos,
now a tourist resort by the A4067 in the valley of the
Tawe. She retired to Craig-y-Nos and died there.
Madame Patti was still enjoying her retirement when the
extraordinary Dan-yr-Ogof show caves across the road
were first explored. But hill-walkers tend to be as
apathetic about caves as most motorists are about all
those bits and pieces under the bonnet.

Brecon, though, is clearly more interesting than it
looked on that dismal evening when I booked in at the
Lansdowne Hotel and discovered an engaging eccentricity: the lights in the reception area were illuminated
by pressing a switch in a telephone box. This can be
disturbing when you are making a call and the receptionist opens the door and fumbles about on the wall behind
you. Moreover, I had unusual companions at dinner: a
businessman from Criccieth who sold nuts and bolts
('special ones') and a young couple from Dallas who
inevitably had something to do with oil. The Americans
had shown more initiative than many of their compatriots
do: instead of staying in London they were touring
Britain in a hired car. For some odd reason they wanted
to know where they could see some steam engines. We
told them to go to York.

You can imagine the combined effect of those off-
putting chats at the mountain centre and the national
park office, the musings about Sarah Siddons and
Adelina Patti, and the encounters with a quaint lighting
system and an oil man looking for steam engines. The
seeds of bewilderment were within me when, next
morning, I set off for the hills. It was misty again and the
drizzle had a remorseless quality that suggested it would
still be falling thus when, that night, I was tucked up in
bed. The rain was no bother but the mist was a nuisance,
because poor visibility is inhibiting when one is doing a
solo over unfamiliar hills and the house is still mortgaged.

(*above*) Metropolitan Police cadets on Huccaby Bridge, Dartmoor; (*below*) Leeden Tor, Dartmoor (*Eric Lumb*)

The River Usk and the Brecon Beacons (*British Tourist Authority*)

To be serious for a minute, there is an international standard which redefines mist as fog when visibility is less than 1 kilometre (about 1,100 yards). For those who crave further information about this grey area I will add two facts. First, rural fogs are cleaner, less dense, than urban fogs. Second, hill fog forms when a moist stream of air cools (as we all do) when it moves upwards. What mattered, as I drove up the wildly attractive Glyn Tarell and parked in a lay-by just past the mountain rescue post that used to be the Storey Arms, was that the mist and drizzle would soon become fog and drizzle.

Those of you who know the area will be aware that, possibly with an excess of prudence, I had chosen the tourist route. This was cheating. I was doing almost half the climb on wheels and was sneaking up on the Brecon Beacons from the back door. Never mind – too much caution is safer than too little, if less exciting. At least I was going to the top and keeping my options open. The weather might clear for an hour or two and, with such luck, who would want to be pacing about restlessly in the valleys? Far better to be on the tops when the curtains were drawn back. I was just putting on my rucksack and slamming the boot of the car when I realised that I was still wearing shoes. My mind was not in gear that morning. Properly socked and booted, I made my way alongside a wood, across a stream, and up a path so badly eroded by thousands of walkers that in places it was like an unmade road. Higher up, the broad track sometimes had the muddy, sloppy consistency of a farmyard after the cows have come home on a wet day. Let me confess to an ambivalent attitude towards paths. It is an exhilarating, richly satisfying experience to plan and follow a route over tracklessly desolate country, especially if it is unfamiliar and one is doing a solo. If there is no path, fine. Make your own way but have the courtesy to stay clear of farmland. At the same time no one wants the countryside to be scarred by more paths than are necessary. The compromise is this: if there is a path going your way, use it. But walk on the path rather than its fringes, because widening a path contributes to the ugly erosion of the natural landscape. If you need proof, climb Pen y Fan the way I did.

A monument commemorated the fact that the Brecon Beacons were given to the National Trust by the Eagle Star Insurance Company in 1965. This inspired mischievous speculation about what an insurance company was doing with them in the first place. The acquisition was, in fact, fortuitous. The Eagle Star have millions of pounds to invest every year and put about 20 per cent of it into properties of one sort or another. In 1957 the executors of Lord Tredegar's estate were selling it and the Eagle Star bought his agricultural land, which included a lot of common land that was not of much use to them. This incorporated the Beacons. The National Trust, concerned about the effects of wear and tear, wanted to take over the management and conservation of the area and therefore asked if they could have it. The Eagle Star agreed. Aptly, the company's chairman at the time was a Mountain (Sir Brian).

The rain seemed to be hovering rather than actually falling. It had the insubstantial wetness that soaks by stealth. Broad, rocky, and unpleasant though it was, the track was reassuring for a stranger to the region – because visibility was soon restricted to about 75 yards, then 50. Not that there was any question of getting lost, any more than there is on a motorway. I did a double-take at some shyly inquisitive sheep because their faces were so neatly, almost delicately formed. Sheep often look cuddly, but seldom hint so strongly at prettiness. The special breed hereabouts are Brecknock Hill Cheviots, a cross between transmigrated Cheviots and the Welsh Mountain breed. The intimately foggy silence was relieved by the small sounds familiar to all hill-walkers: faint birdsong, the occasional, distant drone of traffic, the soft soughing of the wind, the rustle of clothing in motion, the crunch of boots on stony ground.

After an hour I reached a ridge and turned left – that is, north – towards Corn Du (2,863ft or 873m) and Pen y Fan (2,906ft or 886m). And suddenly there was another, momentarily startling sound: muffled shouts. How eerie it was to be up there alone, closely wrapped in fog, listening to distorted human voices with no visible source. Someone in trouble, perhaps, or one of nature's acoustic jokes? No. A moment's thought told me it had to be the Special Air Services or the Parachute Regiment. The SAS, the Army's incognito élite, merge into the background like wallpaper. Experts in armed and unarmed combat, mountain warfare, sabotage and parachuting, they use the Brecon Beacons for exercises in physical and mental endurance, survival techniques, map-reading and compass work, and self-reliance. Recruits to the Parachute Regiment are trained up there, too, in packs harried by noisy NCOs. That day, in spite of the shouting, no bodies emerged from the fog until I had reached the triangulation pillar at the top of Pen y Fan. From the car, this had taken an hour and a quarter. The national park committee's leaflet estimates an hour and a half – presumably for Sunday afternoon family parties. It is unlikely that any adult with two sound legs would make the ascent more slowly than I did, short of taking a nap on the way. For some reason one hip was not functioning as it should. The lubricating juices had dried up. Possibly a recent excess of long-distance driving (too much sitting) had provoked strike action by the internal mechanic who normally greases the ball-bearings. Anyway, I was no contender for speed records.

I was loitering on Pen y Fan, hoping the fog would clear and wondering what to do next if it didn't, when soldiers bearing webbing and rifles burst through the grey curtain between Pen y Fan and Cribin (2,608ft or 795m) down to the east. The morning was riven by such bullying admonitions as 'Don't go that way – you'll fall off' and 'Stay away from that right-hand edge, you blockhead'. Though intimidating in volume and tone, the comments were strangely prim. In my day NCOs explored a limited vocabulary of expletives on such occasions, rather than using decorous words like 'blockhead'. I gave these NCOs credit for moderating their language in the startling presence of a civilian – startling because there was no good reason why any civilian in his right mind should be on Pen y Fan on such a day. When an officer turned up, sporting the familiar cap badge and maroon beret, there was more justification than usual for introductory trivialities about the weather. It was, I suggested, a lousy morning to be up there. But much depended (I recalled Gerard Manley Hopkins' verse in praise of 'wildness and wet') on what one wanted out of life. 'All I want out of life', said that hard-nosed soldier, 'is the weekend.' Here, clearly, was neither poet nor philosopher. He asked where I came from and we noted how odd it was that the only people on Pen y Fan that dreary morning came from the same distant chunk of England: the Paras from Aldershot and the civilian from Seale, a mile or two away on the other side of the Hog's Back. At the time there was a television series about training recruits to the Paras and the previous evening's instalment, he said, had shown them doing exactly what they were doing now – a 15-mile 'long march' over the Brecon Beacons. At first, I told him, I had thought they might be the SAS. Incredulous, he eyed his charges with a suggestion of disgust: 'What, this lot?'

I left them in conference and wandered vaguely down towards Cribin. But it was futile to go on. There was not a glimmer of hope that the fog would clear. Disappointed, I turned and went back the same way: downhill through the mud, the rain and the vaporous gloom. There was much sloshing and thumping of boots as a party of walkers went by in five scattered groups. Some had lost visual contact with the groups in front and behind: in thick fog that was bad hill-craft, even on such an obvious track. I got back to the car after what had been no more than a morning stroll, and removed the note from the windscreen. Briefly, I was tempted to leave it there. A charming vignette presented itself to the eyes of the mind. The car park attendant at Farnham checks such scraps of paper to see if one's time has expired. Imagine his reaction to the information that I had a blue rucksack and was going up Pen y Fan and possibly Cribin and Craig Cwm-llwch and should be back by six . . . With rain beating on the roof, I towelled down, changed into a dry pair of trousers (a challenging contortion within the constricting context of a car), and lunched on soup and wine. That quick trip to the top and back had merely been a loosener, but there was nothing productive to be done with the reserves of time and energy. Some whim induced me to call in at the mountain centre, where the day's weather forecast was pinned on a notice board. It scored three out of three by referring to 'drizzle', 'poor visibility', and 'copious hill fog'. That uncommon word 'copious' was exactly right.

As I pointed the car towards home there was a sudden outburst of sunshine. This example of Sod's Law was momentarily vexing until I looked back towards the tops and saw that they were still thickly cloaked in fog, still keeping their secrets. But what handsome hills they were in their gently harmonious variety of shape and colouring – the latter composed primarily of woodland, bracken, grass and protruding sandstone. It was spring and the lambs were everywhere, some creamy, some black, all of them looking freshly laundered, tidy, like those fluffy and fetching stuffed toys in shop windows. The hills and the lambs: in visual terms, hymns ancient and modern.

You may reasonably wonder why I did not push on in spite of the fog, bagging a few more tops like some acquisitive botanist popping specimens into the can. But what would I have seen anyway? One patch of fog is much like another. And the challenge of route-finding by map and compass in such conditions has long since lost its novelty. Nowadays I expect an adequate reward for such labours. Consider, too, that when unfamiliar and potentially hazardous terrain is shrouded in fog it makes no kind of sense to stick perversely to one's plans for the day, unless accompanied by someone who knows every inch of the way. What a bother it would be for anyone lumbered with the possible chore of finding and bringing back the body. So ignore that nagging thought 'I could have done more'. To a certain extent that should be true of every day's walk. We must stay within the safe limit of our capabilities.

It would be difficult to exaggerate the importance of care and competence in route-planning and navigation. There are three things we need to know: where we are going, how to get there, and the approximate time it will take to do so. If you do not know where you are going you should not be on the hills anyway. In planning a route it is always satisfying to have a 'big' finish: something spectacular but not necessarily exhausting. Assuming you have a choice, it is a good idea to get the most strenuous walking out of the way while you are still fresh. Ideally, I like a gentle ascent for the first half-hour or so while breakfast is settling, and in this respect the foothills are usually obliging. The body should then be ready for a stiff climb and the rest of the day will probably be of intermediate and variable quality in terms of the effort demanded. One of the boons of hill-walking, of course, is that unless camping overnight on the tops we always have a downhill walk at the end of the day, navigating with exemplary concentration towards one of those places identified on the map by the word 'inn'.

Throughout the day, navigation depends on translating the information on the map into the natural features we see around us. If we cannot see any natural features, because of intervening fog, then the ability to use a compass becomes as fundamental as the ability to read a map. More about that later, because avuncular advice is best digested in small doses. For the moment let us assume that we know where we are going and how to get there and can use a map and compass with the facility (well, almost) with which we use a knife and fork. This brings us to the question of an ETA – estimated time of arrival. There are two reasons why we need to be fussy about this, though no one is going to cavil about an hour's margin for error either way. One, it affects our arrangements for the evening – eating, drinking, transport, and so on. Two, if the walk takes hours longer than a too-casual estimate we may cause anxiety to others and, possibly, inconvenience to a rescue party (because if heading for remote places we will have left with some responsible person a detailed note of our intentions). The time a walk takes depends largely on the steepness and difficulty of the terrain. Progress is slow, sometimes very slow, when we are tackling stiff ascents or scrambling about on rocks. The popular formula for estimating the duration of a walk, including modest breaks, is to allow an hour for every 3 map miles and add half an hour for every 1,000ft (305m) climbed. But formulas are too formal for me. I cut out the investigation of contour lines and the ensuing mathematics and merely estimate 2 miles an hour. This works well for normal hill-walking and one soon learns how to adjust the estimate if the map indicates that the going will be abnormally easy or strenuous.

In navigating, we need to know the language on the map when identifying natural features. The basic linguistic challenges in Wales fit roughly into three categories: ups and downs, size, and water. Bryn, carnedd or garnedd, fan or ban, foel, moel, mynydd, pen and twyn all indicate high places. Fan or ban suggests a location where waters gather, foel or moel has connotations of baldness, pen means top, and twyn means hillock. In the same category are bwlch (a pass or saddle between peaks), careg (rock), craig or clogwyn (crag), crib or grib (ridge), cefn (back or ridge), cwm (steep-sided hollow), and rhos (moorland or marsh). Careg often occurs in its plural form, cerrig. For clues about size and position, note that bach, bychan, fach and fechan all refer to a comparative smallness, and that fawr and mawr are comparatively large. The watery words are aber (confluence or estuary), afon (river), llyn (lake), nant (stream or valley), and rhaiadr (waterfall). An acquaintance with that rough-and-ready Welsh glossary eases the hill-walker's task and, moreover, makes the day more interesting. Trite though the English translations may be, what romantic, rousing expressions these are when one sees them scattered across the map from the Black Mountains, plural, to the Black Mountain, singular.

The direct route to Pen y Fan via Cefn Cwm-llwch is no longer hindered by rifle ranges. Probably the best walk, though, is up the Bryn-teg ridge to Cribin and along the tops to the Tommy Jones obelisk (a memorial to a boy of five who died after he had climbed there alone from Cwm-llwch Farm in 1900) and then down via Pen Milan. An attractive alternative from the south is a boomerang route from the Neuadd Reservoirs. Take the Roman road up to the pass known as The Gap and then follow the edge to Cribin, Pen y Fan, Corn Du (a Bronze Age burial ground at a time when the area was wooded), and return to Bwlch Duwynt and the crags of Gwaun-taf and Fan-ddu. You can make your own boomerangs with the help of a national park information sheet available at the mountain centre: but be prepared for some lane-pounding at the Brecon end. Two examples are offered below. And may you bask in sunshine all the way.

Other suggested walks

1 Follow the track west of Bryn up Gist Wen to Craig Cwareli and then turn north-west to the three main tops and descend via the Tommy Jones obelisk and Cwm Llwch.

2 A shorter route ascends the Cefn Cyff to The Gap, Cribin, and Pen y Fan before using the direct line of descent down Cefn Cwm-llwch.

3

Splashing around
Rhinog Fawr

Before heading for the highest bumps on the combined
surface area of England and Wales, it seemed a good idea
to sample one of the less fashionable Welsh ranges. There
was a short list of tempting candidates: the Prescelly Hills
(which have three alternative spellings), Plynlimon, the
Arans, the Berwyns and the Rhinogs. The hill-walking
fraternity, including adventure-training specialists in the
services, spoke of the Rhinogs with a unanimous respect
that combined awe and affection. Indeed, the more I
heard and read about them the more obvious it became
that the Rhinogs were just the thing for any hill-walker
who knew what was what. Rhinog Fawr (2,362ft or
720m), Rhinog Fach (2,333ft or 711m), Y Llethr (2,475ft
or 754m), and Diffwys (2,462ft or 750m) stand in line
from north to south and offer a choice of testing routes –
all of them difficult to navigate – over remote, rocky,
almost trackless terrain. This is a mountainous wilderness, a tangled maze of boulders and bilberries and deep
heather on a shattered landscape. The huge blocks of rock
are so crazily disarranged, the ups and downs so
strenuously unpredictable, the route-finding so difficult,
that the Rhinogs are justly renowned (among the
cognoscenti, anyway) as the toughest, most baffling
walking country in Wales – or England, for that matter.
Except for huge stone walls, some of them 8ft (2.4m) high,
there is hardly a hint that Man has ever passed this way or
ever will. But there was an ancient trade route across
those mountains. The Rhinogs raise echoes, too, of the
Romans, the Napoleonic wars, and one of the most
turbulent periods in Britain's political history. Given all

43

RHINOGS WALK (North Wales)

- - - → Author's route

0 ½ 1 km
0 ½ 1 mile

N

(to Harlech)

Start here
(parking)

Afon Artro

Pen-y-bont

(to Llanbedr)

Ty-croes

Llyn Cwm Bychan

Foel Wen

Glan-rhaiadr

Cwm Nantcol

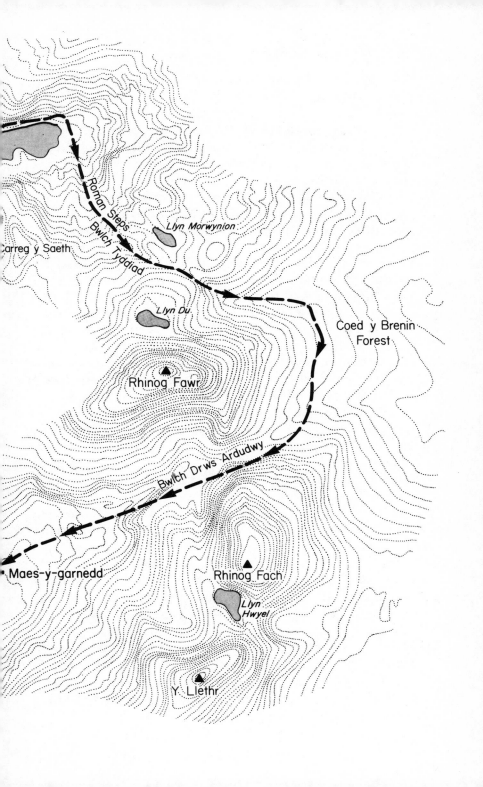

that, plus their botanical splendours and the proximity of Harlech Castle, the Rhinogs have to be rated as one of the best shows outside the West End.

Moreover, should the mountains themselves be hidden away in off-putting fog there is a circular walk around Rhinog Fawr that can serve as a substitute for the big stuff and an introduction to the special character of the entire area. That alternative was important because I was to have as company a friend and his dog, both unknown quantities in a hill-walking context, and wanted to guarantee them an interesting day whatever the weather. On a solo I tend to improvise – a dignified euphemism for muddling through – but on this occasion I was responsible for others and therefore studied the map with particular care. These preparations even included typewritten notes ('Path downhill to east, into woods') that would have done justice to the most formal of guidebooks. Given a clear day we could turn south from Bwlch Tyddiad and, discarding the notes in favour of map and compass, tackle the challenge of both Rhinogs and possibly Y Llethr.

The options thus neatly arranged, the weather forecasts ignored, and accommodation reserved, I collected Nicholas Keith and his four-year-old black labrador. Harris, and set off with a full tank on the road to Harlech. Nicholas had just gone into the publishing business after almost three years as sports editor of *The Times*. There was a lot happening in his life and the man's soul needed refreshment. He was no hill-walker but offered reassuring if bizarre references: he was accustomed to a few ups and downs, he said, because when he had nothing better to do he sometimes went to the island of Shona, in Loch Moidart, and helped to round up sheep. This is not a common practice among Old Etonians (nor sports editors, for that matter) and confirmed what I already knew – that although Nicholas could live with the conventions he was not shackled by them. Moreover he was fit, almost twenty years my junior, and combined two qualities hill-walkers need: initiative and serenity. There

46

are times when hill-walkers also find it necessary to be amphibious and on this count labradors earn high marks. Harris had another, more tenuous affinity with the Rhinogs. The family previously had a dog called Wellington and decided to name the newcomer after one of Wellington's generals, Lord Harris, whose son had a shoulder perforated at Waterloo. That battle marked the end of the Napoleonic wars, which had a lasting effect on the Rhinogs because of the massive stone walls supposedly built by French prisoners. A dog named after a general was therefore, to some extent, maintaining the connection.

We stopped short of Harlech, at Llanbedr. In booking rooms at Cae Nest Hall I had guessed, correctly, that this arboreal refuge would suit our purposes admirably. For a start, there was an attractive, almost naked young lady in the bathroom. She was just a picture on the wall but the owners evidently wanted one's stay to be as agreeable as they could make it. The hotel's cosy, welcoming character was not its only recommendation. The cuisine was imaginatively satisfying and extended, next day, to packed lunches that were models of their kind: chicken legs, sandwiches, hard-boiled eggs, cheese and biscuits, crisps, peanuts, chocolate biscuits, and apples. More than we needed but nevertheless exemplary (and Harris accommodated the left-overs). Norma and David Thomas had taken over Cae Nest Hall only a month earlier, after David had devoted twenty-eight years to the manufacture of printing ink. He had enjoyed making the stuff, he said, but became disenchanted with his eventual, less obviously creative role as technical director. So instead of catering for the professional needs of printers he widened his range, catering for the personal needs of those washed up on the banks of the Artro by the tides of chance.

The Artro is rich in trout. So are the little lakes scattered around the Rhinogs. Botanists can have fun, too, delving into the luxuriant vegetation for unusual

47

mosses and ferns. And note that here, as in similar areas of Wales, the word hafod (plural hafodau) keeps appearing on the map. It indicates the site of huts that provided temporary summer dwellings for the hill-farmers of times long gone. The worsening climate made them turn from arable crops to cattle. Late in the Middle Ages there was increasing trade in livestock between highland Wales and the big fairs of lowland England. But such traffic had been going on for centuries. Llanbedr's 11ft (3.3m) Maen Hir is among the standing stones that remind us of what was probably a Bronze Age trade route that acquired such solid markers at some time between the fifth and seventh centuries. That route over the wild Harlech Dome may have served as a link between Ireland and England. From the Artro estuary it went east of north, to Moel Goedog, and then to Llyn Trawsfynydd, the Vale of Bala, the Berwyns, and Shropshire. These days, the paradox about the northern shore of Llyn Trawsfynydd is that only a mile and a main road separate the Roman settlement of Tomen y Mur from a nuclear power station. The Romans developed many existing prehistoric tracks over the highlands of Britain. One of these, of a later date than the Moel Goedog route to the north, went over Bwlch Tyddiad. And whatever the weather did to us, Nicholas and Harris and I were going the same way.

We drove past the bridge at Pen-y-bont, well known as a starting point for the easiest ascent to the jungle of boulders on Rhinog Fawr, and parked alongside the Artro. The river was bubbling and sparkling in the misty morning light as we walked up the lane past a golden drift of autumn leaves banked against a wall. The variety of colouring in that valley was enchanting and we soon became aware of vague heights to the north-east and south-east: Clip (1,937ft or 590m) and Carreg y Saeth (1,442ft or 439m). I say 'vague' because those heights were sensed rather than seen. The upward view was restricted by a dense greyness. It was also raining. We were not to know it at the time, but we had launched our little expedition during one of those periods of inexorably continuous wetness that lead one to regard rain as a permanent condition, as British as fish and chips. That day, the weather began badly, deteriorated, and never improved. By mid-afternoon I was musing on the fact that I had only once been wetter with clothes on – and that was deliberate. In the days when tennis professionals could still drink I was summoned to join a group of players who, that day, had lost their matches in the United States championships. Reading the signs correctly, I dressed in drip-dry clothing for the inevitably boisterous drinking party in Greenwich Village. The location was about as informal as you can get (the staff emptied ashtrays on the floor) but at some stage of the evening a very large waiter threatened us with ejection unless we 'quit horsin' around'. The point of the drip-dry clothing was that later – much later – all I had to do, to wash the beer stains out of shirt and trousers, was take off my shoes and stand under the shower. On emerging from this cleansing deluge I found a Davis Cup player curled up on the floor and sleeping like a babe. Professional tennis, alas, is not like that any more.

Anyway, there we were, Nicholas and I, pausing by Llyn Cwm Bychan to put on over-trousers and batten everything down while Harris sniffed around and wondered what all the fuss was about. Restless animals, dogs, when let loose on the hills. Philistines, too, immune from even the slightest prickling of the aesthetic senses. Could he not appreciate the striking charm of the environment? Llyn Cwm Bychan is a layer of tranquillity set among steep slopes of heather and bracken, great tiers of rock, and clouds and silence. But Harris kept his head down. To get out of that mountainous yet well-wooded cul-de-sac we turned right, just past the lake, and climbed through an oak wood and across open country to the Roman Steps. At their foot, just out of the wood, a path of sorts rises to Gloyw Lyn and provides access to Rhinog

49

Fawr. But that way was barred by low, thick cloud. A lesser prospect was preferable to no prospect at all, so we took the Roman route. This consists of slabs of unworked rock forming an intermittent stairway. Historians disagree about the origins of the Roman Steps. The likeliest story is that although the route was Roman (using a prehistoric pathway), the steps were not. They were probably laid there much later, during the packhorse era. Whatever the answer, they excite speculation about the traffic that has probably passed this way for more than 2,000 years: and about the men who eventually transformed a pathway into a crude staircase and thus left a lasting legacy for posterity on an otherwise primeval landscape of heather and tumbled boulder scree.

That pass has a savage, exceptional beauty and, except for one short stretch, its craggy flanks are not constricting. Harris had long since realised that this was no routine constitutional. He and Nicholas were doing more than their share of the leading, so we were progressing slightly faster than I usually do in that lazy, contemplative hour after breakfast. We reached Bwlch Tyddiad (1,450ft or 442m), the top of the Roman Steps, after an hour and a half of increasingly wet walking. Those who need the solace of a more substantial watery view can make a short diversion to Llyn Morwynion, 'the lake of the virgins'. Any lake stuck up in the hills at 1,292ft (394m) is reasonably safe from pollution and therefore has virginal connotations. More interesting, and also more frustrating, was the fact that we were now little more than 1,000 'map' yards (900m) and about 1,000ft (300m) from the summit of Rhinog Fawr. But it would not be easy for a hill-walker to find 1,000 tougher yards than these – and all we could see of Rhinog Fawr, hazily, was the broad bulk of its base. The heights were no more than a looming presence in the mist and the mind. The climb to the top, via Llyn Du, would have to wait for a better day.

So we carried on to the east, down across open moorland into the north-western segment of Coed y

(*above*) Rhinog Fawr, Rhinog Fach and Y Llethr, from Cwm Nantcol, North
Wales (*Tom Dodd*); (*below*) From Bwlch Tryfan (Snowdonia), Peter Cuthbert
decides that the icy scree slope to the left of Bristly Ridge can be ascended more
safely than the ridge itself

(*above*) The chaotic jumble of rocks on Glyder Fach, with Snowdon in the distance; (*below*) Wintry view of Snowdon from Glyder Fach

Brenin Forest, and ducked about under tentacular branches before sorting out the regular stream from its transient allies. We squelched down a broad firebreak, turned right on a Forestry Commission road, and sought shelter from the driving rain – because our first refreshing pause of the day was overdue. A refuge was unwittingly provided by the Jones brothers, the Ruthin hauliers. We were – and are – grateful. They had left a vehicle alongside the track and when I reached up and tried the door, the gods were smiling on us. We scrambled in and settled down for lunch. There were only two seats and Harris (whose condition was such that the word 'wet' does not even begin to describe it) decided he would share mine. Dogs are cute that way. They know that a chance acquaintance tends to be a softer touch than an owner when it comes to handing over the goodies. We had just reached the stage of lighting pipes and talking ourselves into the mood for another drenching when a Forestry Commission car arrived. The driver did a double-take. Well, wouldn't you? He had been charging through remote woodland at an altitude of 1,000ft in foul weather, minding his own business, when he was suddenly confronted by two men and a dog gazing at him through the windscreen of an abandoned haulage vehicle. He got out and came over to see us, politely explaining that he had thought we might have come from the hauliers. We invited him in for coffee, which seemed the decent thing to do, and Harris moved over. The formal social observances somehow assume a special importance in such ludicrous situations. Our companion told us that they produced 40,000 tons of timber a year. The logs went to local sawmills and markets and the pulp wood had been going to Scandinavia. The Forestry Commission leased 34 square miles of Coed y Brenin Forest, not all of it planted, and had about 70 full-time employees. They integrated forestry and agriculture, he said, by employing some smallholders. As hill-walkers, he asked, how did we feel about the Forestry Commission? He doubtless knew the answer already. Most of us find natural hardwoods visually more pleasing and far more interesting, because of their variety and the space they leave for daylight. At the same time we appreciate the need for organised, quick-growing commercial woodland, in spite of its distasteful regimentation. It has also reclothed many of our previously denuded uplands and given them a wider range of colouring.

Thus we chattered on until our guest departed and a few warning shivers told us that we had been stationary for too long. During a soggy ascent along the edge of the forest and across the moor to Bwlch Drws Ardudwy we exchanged asides – about the weather, of course – with two groups of walkers. Eccentrics greeting eccentrics with the dry wit that flourishes in wetness. Water on the brain. Bwlch Drws Ardudwy (1,155ft or 352m) is a deep, gloomy cleft between the rugged walls of the Rhinogs. Assuming that you can see what you are doing, Rhinog Fach can be climbed in an hour, whereas from this point Rhinog Fawr is an unreasonably steep and confusing obstacle course. We splashed over the wild but heathery pass. Every sloping groove in the surface was a watercourse of some kind, and the white scars of temporary falls rippled down the hillsides. 'There's one down my back, too,' said Nicholas, who was walking on water – or through it, anyway – as nonchalantly as the imperturbable Harris. It occurred to me that after a day's hill-walking like this, it would take a blizzard to impress them. The wind and rain were relentless but at least we were going downhill and in the general direction of Cae Nest Hall, the young lady on the bathroom wall, and dry clothes.

But the first solid structure we came to, other than the flanking tiers of rock, was the dark and sturdy farmstead of Maes-y-Garnedd. This has an ambiguous place in history as the birthplace (and it has not changed much since) of Colonel John Jones. During the Civil War he served in the parliamentary forces and earned high marks

54

for the odd achievement of twice suppressing resistance on Anglesey. Between these two militant excursions across the Menai Strait he found time to be returned to the Long Parliament as Member for Merionethshire. He was sailing along with hardly a care in the world, but committed himself in two directions that initially promised fair winds but ultimately wrecked him. One, he married Oliver Cromwell's third sister, Catherine. Two, he was selected as one of the judges of Charles I, diligently attended the trial, and signed the death warrant that, in 1649, cost the king his head. For a time, all continued to go well for the able Jones. He helped to govern Ireland. He was summoned to the Protector's House of Lords. But two years later, in December 1659, he was arrested and impeached for high treason because he had quarrelled with Parliament while commanding Irish forces. They released him when he promised to behave himself and toe the government line. But in 1660 the Restoration (Charles II) left him up the creek without a paddle. He was Cromwell's brother-in-law and, moreover, had taken what was now an unpopular party line. The lad from Maes-y-Garnedd was arrested again and popped in the Tower. He was executed in October 1660, but died with dignity. Colonel Jones, regicide, hero and villain in turn, was buried in the churchyard at Llanenddwyn, little more than two miles down the road from Llanbedr. There are many trite morals to be drawn from this reminder that a high proportion of eminent people have obscure origins. Perhaps the most relevant moral for this book is that those who walk in high places must take care with their footwork.

We plodded along the winding, undulating lane down Cwm Nantcol (far too much road work) and eventually reached the attractively wooded confluence of rivers and lanes at Ty-croes and had a last drag up the Artro to the car. It was still raining. We were disappointed only in that the weather had denied us a longer, more strenuous day and wider, higher views. But hill-walkers, like mountaineers, succeed in life – on a small scale, anyway – every time they complete a planned route over unfamiliar terrain. We had walked about 13 map miles in just over 5 hours, plus almost an hour and a half devoted to two assaults on those packed lunches (on the last stretch we briefly sheltered in a deserted cattle-shed). Back at Cae Nest Hall, my morning note about our proposed route and fine-weather options seemed ridiculously optimistic when re-read. David Thomas told us that the cloud had never been so low in his entire month as landlord. 'If you'd been a week earlier you'd have had no problems. Very clear.' The words sounded like an echo of my elderly adviser at the Brecon Beacons mountain centre. This time we had at least had a good stretch.

The fact remains that we had walked round Rhinog Fawr rather than over it. The tops had retained their mysteries, closely wrapped. We had merely been soaked and gently exercised, rather than confused and exhausted. Five months after that round tour with Nicholas and Harris, I happened to be in North Wales again and hoped that, on the way home from Betws-y-Coed, I might sneak up on the Rhinogs and catch them off guard. But the scene at Llyn Cwm Bychan was unchanged – wind and rain, low, heavy cloud, and damply thoughtful sheep. Rhinogs 2, Rex Bellamy 0. But the match isn't over yet.

Other suggested walks

1 A long and tiring boomerang walk from Cwm Bychan could take in the Roman Steps and Bwlch Tyddiad, Llyn Du, Rhinog Fawr, Bwlch Drws Ardudwy, Rhinog Fach, Y Llethr, Cwm Nantcol and Gloyw Lyn.
2 A smaller boomerang from Cwm Bychan follows a path north-east to Bwlch Gwylim and then swings south-east along the eastern shore of Llyn Pryfed before returning (with much difficulty) to Bwlch Tyddiad and Cwm Bychan.

4

A Gymnast's Guide to the Glyders

---◆---

Cader Idris, 'Arthur's Chair', lies south of the Rhinogs and Dolgellau; but its visual splendours have a spiritual and physical affinity with the mountains gathered around Pen-y-Gwryd in the heart of Snowdonia. There is a myth that anyone who spends a night on Cader Idris will wake up blind, mad, or poetic. The grain of truth tucked away in this fancy is that a man must be blind or mad if Cader Idris does not bring out the poet that lurks within all of us. In Snowdonia itself there is much to be said in favour of the grassy Carnedds and the Moel Siabod range (less crowded than the more celebrated mountains). But the two great challenges for the hill-walker who can take some airy scrambling in his stride are the renowned 'horseshoe' routes: Tryfan, Bristly Ridge, Glyder Fach and Y Gribin, or Crib Goch, Snowdon and Y Lliwedd. If done the hard way, both demand a head for heights and a rudimentary knowledge of rock-climbing. But both horseshoes can be sampled via less hair-raising options and one of these is described here. It did not include Snowdon – we can discuss that later – but its variety was an unfailing stimulus to the senses, its views superb, and (for a hill-walker, anyway) its technical challenges absorbing.

Chris Brasher, writer, runner, mountaineer, and all-purpose dynamo, knows North Wales far better than I ever will. Where would his fancy take him, I asked, if he was granted one day's leave from the next world to come back to this one for some exhilarating hill-walking in Snowdonia? The word 'walking' was given particular weight because I wanted to keep my feet on the ground, rather than submit to any prolonged dependence on the

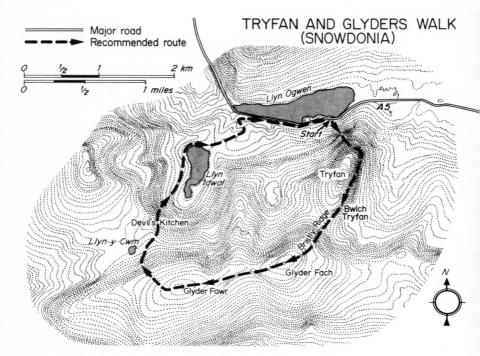

Major road
Recommended route

0   ½   1   2 km
0   ½   1 miles

Llyn Ogwen

A5

Start

Llyn Idwal

Tryfan

Bwlch Tryfan

Devil's Kitchen

Bristly Ridge

Llyn-y-Cwm

Glyder Fach

Glyder Fawr

N

adhesive qualities of fingers and toes. The man's answer
was instant, because he is not the kind to go into
committee before making up his mind. Go to Llanberis,
he said, and then amble over the Glyders, Bristly Ridge
and Tryfan (I ignored a playful aside about the Milestone
Buttress). He added the reassuring rider that there was no
climbing to do: just some easy scrambling. I pushed aside
a suspicion that Chris Brasher's conception of 'easy
scrambling' might differ from mine. And neither of us
was to know that when I tackled a reversed amendment of
his route in the company of the Metropolitan Police, the
rocky heights would be smeared with verglas disguised
under light falls of graupel, and March winds would be
bustling across the tops – that, in short, the mountains
would be in an interesting condition.

Verglas is treacherous because this thin coating of
wind-blown ice merely makes the rocks look wet. Graupel
is soft hail, differing from true hail in that graupel
does not bounce. It consists of small, loosely attached

58

particles of frozen cloud that look like large white coffee granules and, from a distance, can easily be mistaken for snow. Verglas and graupel are not much fun, especially on top of one another. Given all that, plus the fact that even in the best of weather this is no route for softies, it was inevitable that at times the day would be a strenuous test of mind and muscle. But Chris had chosen wisely. That combination of walk and scramble was richly rewarding. And the 'old man' of the team still had plenty of petrol in the tank – which was as it should be – when we sauntered down to the terminus of Ogwen Cottage for some potentially scalding tea.

Mind you, I was as pampered as a man can be, unless attached to a rope and hauled about like a sack of potatoes. During our merry evening in the Three Crowns at Chagford, Tim Potts had kindly suggested a further rendezvous in North Wales. Thus it was that I turned up at Betws-y-Coed and checked in at the rambling old mansion the police use as a base for adventure training. In residence with the cadets – six girls and eight boys, all preparing for the Dartmoor 10 Tors Expedition – were four 'staff': Tim, Derek Fanning (another acquaintance from Dartmoor), Peter Cuthbert and Barbara Stead. Over drinks at the Gwydyr Hotel it transpired that the arrangements for the following day were heavily loaded in my favour. While Tim and Barbara looked after the cadets, Peter and Derek were to provide supervisory companionship for an eccentric tennis writer with an insatiable enthusiasm for high places. Peter is bearded, has bulging muscles, and confesses to origins in Dundee. Formerly a gymnast, trampolinist and rugby player, he then gravitated towards mountaineering because Nature had clearly designed him for it. Derek, an enviably fit all-round sportsman, modestly implied that his education in hill-walking had not yet been extended to scrambling up and down mountains in wintry conditions. Anyway, they were good lads with well-tuned muscles. There was just one nagging doubt at the back of my mind: was it wise to engage in an exercise suggested by a former Olympic steeplechase champion and led by a former gymnast?

It was a white morning. The bright, blank layer of graupel enhanced the grandeur of the mountains by an illusory exaggeration of their height and girth. We parked by Llyn Ogwen and walked through breeze-blown graupel to the foot of Tryfan's north ridge. Tryfan is the beginner's mountain: and as benign to the rusty as it is to the raw. True, it cannot be climbed unless you lay hands on it; but the holds are always rough and always ready and never let you down. They come in all shapes and sizes, constant only in their abundance. This is not to say that every way up Tryfan is an easy way. The climbing routes are admirably diverse in their degrees of difficulty – which means that the finger-and-toe specialists can move up from class to class in the same school (Tryfan) as they become more proficient. In good conditions Tryfan is just as accommodating for the hill-walker. It is, in short, everybody's mountain – and looks the part, too. This majestic pyramid stuck alongside the A5 rises to 3,010ft (917m), has inviting corrugations on every flank, and boasts not merely one peak but three. Nature even anticipated man's need for a summit marker (usually a cairn) by installing there two parallel 10ft pillars of rock known as Adam and Eve, though no one knows which is which because they lack the necessary distinguishing features. Tradition has it that to stride from one to the other is to gain the freedom of Tryfan, whatever that may mean. Tucked away in some cranny of rock beneath them is a community of mice, who presumably live well on the edible debris left up there by litter-louts. How the mice got to the top of Tryfan in the first place is another story. Were they carried, or did they walk? Anyway, Tryfan is the most impressively striking mountain in Wales, falling short of perfection of form only because of its proximity to the even higher Glyder Fach (3,262ft or 994m).

It soon became clear, as we set about the north ridge, that the order of our going had been prearranged. Peter and Derek were using the carrot-and-stick system. Peter's role was to lead, at a reasonable pace, pausing occasionally until I almost caught him up – whereupon he set off again. Note that this is sound practice for a leader: he must never let his No. 2 feel deserted but nor must he give his No. 2 an excuse to stop. Derek's job, which involved a detailed but irrelevant examination of my boots and breeches, was to kick me up the backside if I showed any tendency to dawdle – or, in the event of a slip, to stamp on me before I gathered momentum. He never (quite) needed to do either and, indeed, complimented me on my footwork and thus raised the possibility that he might have a future as a psychologist.

With the unknown quantity sandwiched between two safe bets, we made our way up some 800ft (240m) of the north ridge. Peter then offered me the choice of staying on the ridge or traversing across to the easier Heather Terrace. He knew that (about halfway up) the ridge narrowed, cast off its clothing of grass and heather, and became altogether more demanding. What he did not know was that I knew it too. So far, in spite of the graupel and the hints of ice, the going had been easy and I had enjoyed the reminder of a vanished youth. But had I still the strength and stamina to see us through what promised to be a taxing day? After the age of forty or thereabouts (certainly after the age of fifty), a little self-doubt sets in: a slight, gradual erosion of confidence in one's physical resources. The important thing is to keep something in the bank. It is the same in most of the conventional sports. The successful are those who know how to pace themselves through a match and ensure that, until it is over, they always have reserves that can be drawn on should the need arise. This discreet line of thinking may have arisen from an excess of prudence, but it indubitably led us to the Heather Terrace. Full marks to Peter for giving me the choice. There are circumstances in which the weakest member of a party, the best judge of his own abilities, must make a decision that affects everyone.

The traverse, in fact, had its moments. There were a few icicles about and on some rocks and steep banks of vegetation thin curtains of ice had formed – as delicately traced as muslin, or morning dew on cobwebs. And Peter led us across a slab that demanded careful balance and footwork. With a twinkle in his eyes he looked over his shoulder to see how I was managing. I paused in mid-air and, with mock reproach, accused him of being deliberately mischievous. He did not contest the point but just grinned and told me: 'I thought you'd find that interesting.' These Scots did not invent understatement, but they developed it to the ultimate point of refinement. We looked down on climbers at the foot of Little Tryfan and at aircraft bursting down the valley of the Llugwy – a sideshow that was even more spectacular when we reached Bwlch Tryfan and saw them swinging sharply round the corner into Nant Ffrancon, 'the valley of beavers'. We looked down, too, on three lakes: Bochlwyd, Idwal and Ogwen. We looked down because there was no longer much to see if we looked up.

Bwlch Tryfan is the dip between Tryfan and Bristly Ridge, the north-eastern spur of Glyder Fach. Bristly Ridge is narrower than the north ridge of Tryfan but no more difficult. Peter decided that, because of the verglas, we should ascend the scree on Bristly's south-eastern flank rather than tackle the ridge itself. That steep scree, coated in ice as it was, turned out to be desperately tiring for a half-fit man in his fifties. There was no question of pausing for the occasional breather, because nobody in his right mind risks loss of momentum when climbing a sheet of ice set at the same angle as the roof of a house. A few rocks protruded, but that scree was bad news and the sooner it was behind us the better. The relentless strain on legs and lungs had me panting for breath and in some distress. And always one had to think in terms of balance. If you play squash you know that it is possible to stay on court for an hour, without too much bother, if playing at an easy pace – but that anyone in a higher class can reduce you to exhaustion in five minutes. Similarly, that scree slope was too much for me – and goodness knows how Derek was coping. He was more than fit enough to deal with the physical challenge, but I suspect that such technical difficulties in an exposed situation were alien to his experience. He also had to keep an eye on me. At the top, Peter admitted that the scree had been a 'borderline' exercise. 'If that ice had been any worse, I'd have aborted.' As a final note on that awful experience, let me point out that – because everything was frozen solid – we went up in single file. The usual drill for any party on a scree slope is to go up or down in a lateral line, so that any displaced rocks will hit no one on the way down. You cannot be sure, of course, that there is nobody else out of sight below you. So take great care to leave all those loose rocks more or less where you found them.

Llyn Ogwen and the Land Rover were memories only 2 hours and 50 minutes old when we reached the chaotic jumble of rocks that is the summit of Glyder Fach. On Dartmoor such disordered assemblies of boulders are known as 'clitter'. The word 'Glyder' is in the same family. The best-known oddity on Glyder Fach is the huge Cantilever Stone (far more securely balanced than it appears to be), which provokes images of diving-boards. During a windswept, 25 minute lunch break we admired a breathtaking panorama that may be the finest in Wales, especially when embellished – as it was then – by a luminous whiteness. We were standing on one of Snowdonia's famous horseshoe scrambles and looking at the other (Crib Goch, Snowdon and Y Lliwedd). If that cliché about having the best of both worlds still means anything, it means such moments as we enjoyed that day amid the patches of sunlight shifting between those great horseshoes and the intervening depths of Llanberis Pass. By contrast with all that sober grandeur, the spiky outcrop of Castell y Gwynt ('Castle of the Winds'), on which rock-climbers can have some fun, was something of a visual joke, a cartoon character amid a cast of 'heavies'.

It was too cold to hang about for long. On the periphery of our view we had noted with curiosity the seemingly drunken lurches of walkers coming our way from Glyder Fawr (3,279ft or 999m). They warned us that it was a slippery crossing. It was indeed. It is not unreasonable to suggest that when leeward is also downward (a steep 1,850ft or 564m to Llyn Cwmffynnon), walking on sloping ice in a strong lateral wind is not a practice to be recommended. I have never acquired a knack for that sort of thing and do not intend to. The circumstances were baffling rather than alarming, but potentially this was one of the many short cuts to life's ultimate terminus. The bafflement arose from an awareness that I simply did not know how to proceed safely in such conditions: and to proceed in any other way would have been to court the possibility of a helter-skelter toboggan run without a toboggan. That would have been a nuisance for all of us. My experience of walking on ice in mountain winds was minimal and more than thirty years out of date. In any case I had in those days been reassured by a layer of metal fixative – crampons or the old-fashioned clinker nails – between boots and ice. The modern rubbery soles have many advantages but on slippery surfaces inspire less confidence than clinkers.

Anyway, the gusts were sometimes powerful enough to shift a man's body weight but were so inconstant that one had to be wary of the temptation to lean into them. You guess? Yes, I dropped through a momentarily unresisting wind, and assumed a recumbent posture. Perplexed, I stayed down for the equivalent of a boxer's mandatory count, trying to work out what was – or should be – going on. In different circumstances I would have lit a contemplative pipe, considered the problem at leisure, and perhaps made a few notes. Peter eyed me gravely, like a doctor uncertain whether he was examining a case of injury, exhaustion, funk, bewilderment or plain malingering. Diagnosing some form of mental paralysis and perhaps guessing that bewilderment was closest to the mark, he kicked an inviting step to get me going again and suggested I keep as upright as possible. The mind in gear again, I realised that waiting for the wind to abate would be futile and that – as on that scree slope – a balanced, controlled momentum was essential.

As we hurried along, Peter voiced a few memory-jogging extracts from the primer that affects all those who walk on ice or frozen snow. The trick, he said, was to use the tread of the boots for purchase: to kick in with the toes when going upwards, with the heels when going downwards, and with the sides of the boot soles (with a sawing action) when going across a slope. The snag about this sound theory is that its practice – kicking into a hard surface – demands strength and energy in the lower leg, and my stock of such commodities had been diminished by that slippery scramble up the scree on Bristly Ridge. In short, the calf muscles no longer had much punch in them and consequently I was not getting enough purchase.

That fleeting incident has been described in some detail so that those of you unfamiliar with its like will be better prepared than I was. Hill-walkers seldom have to answer such posers but it is as well to have a basic education in the nature of mountains in winter. To learn more than we probably need to know is to take out a form of insurance. This is primarily a walker's book but its range is wide and the Glyders expedition is not recommended, in any weather, for those who want to keep their hands in their pockets all day. At times it treads that vague frontier between scrambling and climbing. This frontier need not be feared, but must be respected. Rock-climbing and mountaineering (including the problems set by ice and snow) are specialised crafts and should not be lightly attempted. You may be a competent bricklayer but that does not mean you can build houses. So do not be misled by the fact that in this book you find references to rock-climbing and ascents on snow and ice. My modest knowledge of both (though in youth I was accustomed to rock-climbing, on relatively easy pitches) was acquired in the company of men who knew their stuff. Any hill-walker takes a little scrambling in his or her stride. By 'scrambling' I mean the occasional use of the hands for balance or support, as if using the handrail up a staircase. But if the hands are an essential means of upward or downward progress, if fingers and toes are clinging to holds on rock that even faintly approximates to the vertical, then you are not scrambling – you are climbing. And if you are climbing, especially on snow or ice, you need to know what you are doing or to benefit, during the learning process, from an expert's advice and knowledge of safety procedures.

If we ignore the difference between courage, which is admirable, and foolhardiness, which is silly, we put at risk not only our own lives but possibly those of the mountain rescue services who may have to find us and carry us back. These volunteers do not need the chore of turning out at all hours to search for damaged fools and deliver them to hospital or mortuary. I have taken part in only one mountain rescue. After some thirty-five years the exact location escapes me but, coincidentally, it was either on or near the Glyders. On a summer day a few friends and I had a joyous combination of walk and scramble over a route similar to that described here. We had just begun our descent and were looking forward to supper and a few lubricating pints when some poor chap, one of a large party, fell down a scree slope. He bounced a few times on the way, his body describing ever lower arcs as it flew from one impact to the next. He should have been killed but, incredibly, was detained in hospital at Bangor for only a week. The point is that the business of fetching a mountain rescue team – from Ogwen, as I remember – and helping them with the painstaking, necessarily gentle stretcher-bearing (often a few inches at a time) took seven hours. Yes, seven hours. And one of our number, who was a little older than the rest of us and had assumed a great deal of responsibility, was later to be seen sobbing quietly into his soup. The prolonged mental stress had finally got to him and at that time he was not to know that the victim would recover. In short, mountain rescue is complicated, time-consuming, strenuous, harrowing and often hazardous. It can cost much in both human and material terms.

There were two other lessons we learned from that rescue. One was the possibly critical importance of a basic knowledge of first aid in such circumstances: for example, keep the victim still and warm, making no attempt to straighten broken limbs, but perhaps providing a hot drink (not alcohol, which does not mix well with anaesthetics). The other was the effect of accumulated fear. It transpired, if we correctly interpreted subsequent reports, that the young man who fell was unaccustomed to scrambling about on rocks in high places and, that day, had probably been subjected to more of it than his nerves could take. It seems that eventually he just blacked out – fainted. Whatever the psychological details (and there has been much study of this fascinating theme, especially in times of war), the mind certainly reacts in strange ways when exposed to a prolonged apprehension of danger. Fortitude, or courage, is a form of mental energy. The supply is limited and when it is used up we are in trouble unless the stock is quickly replenished by rest and refreshment. To put it another way, fortitude is like a bank balance. If we keep on spending, signing cheques, there comes a time when we go into the red unless something is paid in.

The shattered rocks at the summit of Glyder Fawr, the highest point of our route, were too much of a mess to be interesting in themselves but commanded beautifully dramatic prospects. There was no longer any way to go but down. Peter chose the cairned path to little Llyn y Cwm, via an occasionally icy scree of small rocks that, even to the untrained eye, had only a remote family connection with the boulders on the ridge above. The long spine of the Glyders is composed of three different types of rock – and, lower down, this diversity is reflected in the vegetation on Clogwyn y Geifr, the crag above the Devil's Kitchen and Llyn Idwal. So if your party includes a geologist, a botanist, or both, prepare yourself to be patient while they roam about and garrulously indulge their fancies. But keep them under close surveillance. You know how careless such enthusiasts can be, once their passions are roused, about such adjacent trivia as 300ft (91m) drops.

The top of the rocky pathway that descends south-east of the notoriously wet chasm known as the Devil's Kitchen is not easy to pick out. Peter's aim was unerring but I have a friend, less familiar with the area, who says that on his first visit he missed the path and had to climb every inch of the way down: and when he said climb, he did not mean scramble. Luckily he was competent in the craft. Such an error could do the average hill-walker incurable harm. We came across more of those delicately pretty curtains of ice on little falls and grassy banks, and at the bottom of the Devil's Kitchen Peter turned to warn us that rocks which looked wet were, in fact, clothed in verglas. Glacial erosion took a chunk out of the northern face of the Glyders to provide a back wall for the depression containing Llyn Idwal. The Devil's Kitchen looked nasty and interested me less than the contiguous vertical fissure, which had long been familiar (in the mind's eye, anyway) from that brilliantly witty essay, C. E. Montague's 'In Hanging Garden Gully'. That joyous extravaganza is largely based on the presence hereabouts of some unusual flora, notably *Lloydia serotina.* Otherwise known as mountain spiderwort, this is found nowhere else in Britain except on Snowdon. Plants may not look all that smart but these locations suggest that *Lloydia serotina* has a highly developed aesthetic sense.

We scrambled and clumped down the maze of rocks between the Devil's Kitchen and Llyn Idwal. Peter slipped gently onto his bum and Derek and I paid for our

68

(*above*) Waterfall in Abbey Brook, Derwent Dale, Peak District; (*below*) Middleton Dale from Curbar Edge, Peak District

(*above*) On the western flank of Pen-y-Ghent, Yorkshire; (*below*) Ingleborough from Twisleton Scars, Yorkshire. The huge boulder was moved to its odd location during the Ice Age (*Tom Parker*)

banter by doing exactly the same, as if victims of a ricochet. Thus was dishonour satisfied, all round. We paused for a few minutes to look at the famous Idwal Slabs, which were designed by Nature – in one of her better moods – for the instruction and pleasure of many generations of rock-climbers. His responsibilities behind him, Peter relaxed and offered terse snippets of his acquired wisdom about rock-climbing and hill-craft in general – about the importance, for example, of going back whenever the route ahead was hazardously vague. 'You've got to keep your brain in gear all the time.' We walked round the western shore of Llyn Idwal. Tradition has it that a young and presumably very naughty Prince Idwal was drowned here by his foster-father and that, consequently, birds would not fly over the lake because they found the scene of the atrocity intimidating. Birds are evidently less credulous than we are when it comes to respecting such legends. But this nature reserve is a wild, rather gloomy place, with the still waters of the lake set at 1,200ft (366m) amid a horseshoe of soaring crags. We followed the tumbling stream down to that renowned climbing base, Ogwen Cottage, which has been so thoroughly modernised that the heroes of the sport's youth would hardly recognise it.

We stood there sipping hot tea among young men toting ice axes. Hill-walkers should not need these but a basic knowledge of their function does us no harm. There had been moments, that day, when they would have been useful. On ice or frozen snow it is not always possible to kick steps. In such circumstances the walker trespasses on the mountaineer's preserve and needs an ice axe for cutting steps, stopping a slide, or probing the depth and consistence of the snow. The spike or pick is for cutting steps in ice, the blade for cutting steps in snow. Hack out a zigzag route up the slope and note that, in order to accommodate both feet, it is necessary to cut a second step above the first before resuming lateral progress. The cutting technique is painstaking, tiring and calls for much practice. To stop a slide, turn on your face and dig the pick into the ice or snow. Need I add that you should hold the axe firmly? If you have no axe, lie on your back and thrust your heels and (if possible) fingers into the slope in the hope of finding a few points of adhesion. Alternatively, pack a parachute and a Bible.

We strolled up the road by Llyn Ogwen (well known for its trout and eels), which rests between the Glyders and the Carnedds, the most northerly mountains in Wales. We were back in the Land Rover after six hours. But our various breaks had added up to almost an hour, so we had taken about five hours to cover roughly – very roughly, in places – six map miles. That slippery scree slope on Bristly Ridge had been the only part of the day's scramble to make unreasonable demands on the second man's strength and energy, though the entire north ridge of Tryfan, plus the direct route up Bristly Ridge, would doubtless have done so. Peter and Derek had kindly adjusted their pace to mine, so I was still going well when we breasted the tape at Ogwen. Derek was so full of running that, back at Betws-y-Coed, he changed into something more appropriate and went for a trot round the village. This was not bravado. He happened to be competing in a half-marathon two days later and did not want to miss his training. You know what these sportsmen are. Always on the boil. Meantime I put it to Peter that he had been boldly indulgent in leading a man of my age and uncertain resources on such an expedition in such conditions. 'Not really,' he said. 'I'd been told that you were fit and competent.' All this was light-hearted but served as a reminder that fitness and competence are relative terms. They probably apply to you and to me in the normal course of hill-walking but may be more difficult to justify on the Glyders jaunt, which can ask interesting questions – even if one takes the easier options – when the conditions fall short of perfection.

That gratifying day on the tops was like rummaging about among faded old photographs, because I had roamed over the Glyders, the Carnedds and Snowdon in 1949. Thanks to Tim Potts and Peter and Derek, active service in Snowdonia was resumed under the watchful protection of good companions. Thus do the young humour the whims of their elders. The fact remains that newcomers to the land the Welsh call Eryri ('Eagles' Nest') may regard the tallest mountain in Wales or England as a more urgent priority.

The uncharitable joke about Snowdon (3,559ft or 1,085m) is that it is the highest slum in Europe. Do not let that put you off. True, its once proud and lonely summit is marred by the sordid accessories of human traffic. The creature comforts include a restaurant and the terminus of a mountain railroad that climbs from Llanberis. Opened in 1896, this remarkable feat of engineering was equipped with engines incorporating the secret of eternal youth. And who are we to say, noses in the air, that such peaks should be reserved for those who can reach them under their own steam? 'Athletic snobs' are no better than the rest of the breed. Consider that one day you and I may still have a yearning for high places, even when legs and lungs can no longer pump us up the intervening slopes. What a boon that railroad would be then. What a glorious whiff of vanished yesterdays we would take in with the wine and the view from Yr Wyddfa. Meantime, while the blood is still hot in the veins (well, warm anyway) remember what a great adventure that railroad must be for those who have never been on a mountain and are curious, and excited, about what it may have to say to them. So let us not be patronising, just because we are luckier, about all the good folk who reach the top by mechanical means. Let us share their pleasure instead of questioning whether they have earned it.

The railroad is not, in any case, the sole source of the tide of humanity that often engulfs the summit of Snowdon. Far from it. There are times when the mountain is almost an ant hill, with rock-climbers draped across the crags like Christmas decorations and walkers plodding up and down a wide variety of access routes like armies on the march. Ignoring the taxing horseshoe of Crib Goch, Snowdon and Y Lliwedd, which is no expedition for mere walkers, the popular paths can best be noted in an anti-clockwise sequence. To the north-west, more or less, is the easiest but least interesting approach, from Llanberis. This seldom strays far from the railroad. To the west is the Snowdon Ranger Path (the oldest) from Llyn Cwellyn, via Clogwyn du'r Arddu. Lower down the clock is a choice of tracks from Rhyd-ddu, Pitt's Head or Beddgelert. South of south-east is the respected Watkin Path from Nant Gwynant, which is embellished by rhododendrons and waterfalls but has a steep finish. To the east, from Pen-y-Pass or Pen-y-Gwryd, are two tough but grand routes that eventually converge. One is the Pig Track, which has no connection with pork. The name is a corruption of PYG (Pen-y-Gwryd). The other, the Miners' Track from Llyn Llydaw, passes disused copper mines. These notes identify what could be described as the beaten tracks and they will suffice for our purposes.

Walking the tops in this area is by no means restricted to those mighty horseshoes dominated by the Glyders and Snowdon. The Carnedds and Moel Siabod, too, are mere samples from the riches of Snowdonia. And if this was a book about afternoon strolls for the family one could go on about the diversity of pretty places to be seen around the tourists' village of Betws-y-Coed ('Sanctuary in the Wood'), which is set among woods and water and hills at the confluence of the Llugwy and the Conwy. For hill-walkers, though, Betws-y-Coed should be regarded as a base rather than a terminus. So should the mountain centre of Capel Curig (Curig was a recluse and a saint), which is snugly ensconced among a soaring crescent of famous peaks fanning out to the north, west and south. There could hardly be a better environment for the Plas y Brenin national centre for mountain activities, and its courses in hill-craft, climbing, canoeing and skiing.

It is difficult to have a clear perspective of a mountain range if one happens to be standing on a chunk of it. Luckily the A5 gives everyone a chance to sniff the bouquet of the wine served in this chapter. Drive from Capel Curig to Bethesda and back again (there are parking places on the way) and marvel at the majesty, south and west of your route, of the continuous 7-mile stretch of peaks, broken up by projecting ridges that reach out towards you as if in welcome. And if you still have the right stuff in you, there will be another day – and this time you will get out of the car, put your boots on, and try Tryfan for size. First, of course, you will have rounded up some chums, strong in mind and muscle, who know their way around. And behave yourself: there may be bobbies about.

Other suggested walks

1 The southern approach to the Glyders, up the Miners' Track from Pen-y-Gwryd, heads towards Tryfan but, west of Llyn y Caseg-fraith, swings left to Glyder Fach and Glyder Fawr and then back to Pen-y-Gwryd via Llyn Cwmffynnon.

2 One of many routes over the Carnedds begins at Llanfairfechan and takes in Carreg Fawr, Drum, Foel Fras, Foel Grach and both Carnedds, then turning north-west from Carnedd Dafydd to Bethesda.

3 From Minffordd on the A487, the main section of Cader Idris can be walked clockwise – the ridge south of Llyn Cau, then Pencoed Pillar, Craig Cau, Penygadair and Mynydd Moel, and back to Minffordd.

5
Edging towards Chatsworth

———◆———

The Peak District lies at the southern extremity of England's highlands and, consequently, is enviably rich in the contrasts that mark any transition from upland to lowland scenery. The most obvious of these is the striking proximity of barren gritstone moors and pretty limestone dales, and the flora and fauna appropriate to each. The beauty of the area is enhanced by its rivers, notably the Derwent, the Wye, and the Dove, and by reservoirs that drowned farming settlements but replaced them with soothing waters. Moreover, the Peak District is remarkable for its social, political, industrial and literary history: much of which will be evident to even the most casual visitor. Whatever the walker's preferences, the Peak District can probably satisfy them. Kinder Scout and Bleaklow are wild moorlands rising over 2,000ft (610m). The scope for ridge walks is modest, though the short stretch from Mam Tor to Lose Hill, between the Hope Valley and the Vale of Edale, is of special interest. And the Peak District excels in the kind of edges that exercise a magnetic allure for rock-climbers and offer the rest of us delightfully panoramic views from the tableland of the moors. The best such walk, all the way from the awful wilderness of the Derwent's source to the tamed, palatial magnificence of Chatsworth, is the subject of this chapter. It begins amid shepherds and still-fresh memories of flooded communities, digresses to a village renowned for Little John and Jane Eyre, passes the graves of seventeenth-century plague victims, and ends within sight of the one-time home of Mary Queen of Scots. It will also keep you out of mischief from dawn till dusk, or near enough.

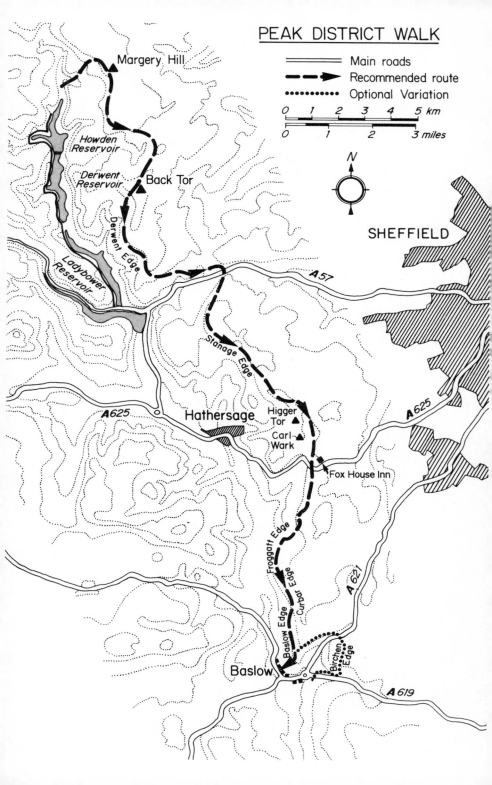

PEAK DISTRICT WALK

	Main roads
	Recommended route
	Optional Variation

0 1 2 3 4 5 km
0   1   2   3 miles

N

Margery Hill

Howden Reservoir

Derwent Reservoir

Back Tor

Ladybower Reservoir

Derwent Edge

SHEFFIELD

A57

Stanage Edge

A625

Hathersage

Higger Tor

Carl Wark

Fox House Inn

A625

Froggatt Edge

Baslow Edge

Curbar Edge

A621

Birchen Edge

Baslow

A619

A series of edges extend from Margery Hill (north-east of Howden Reservoir) to Baslow and Chatsworth Park. They cover 22 or 25 map miles, the difference arising from an optional variation just north of Chatsworth. The map tells you that the walk could begin at Langsett and take in Mickleden Edge on the way to Margery Hill. My objections to including that pleasant tramp in this itinerary are that it increases the transport problems, is somewhat out of character with the rest of the walk, and fits more suitably into other routes. The transport problem is particularly relevant. Nothing could be more logical than to ramble along the entire length of a series of crags laid end to end as if for that very purpose. The only impediment is that such a walk is inevitably linear. Unless a friend is prepared to take you to the start and reel you in at the finish, you must use the two-car system. This is time-consuming. It means that first of all you and your companions must drive in two cars to Baslow, perhaps the evening before the walk, and park one car there. Then drive together in the other car to the top of Derwent Dale. Having thus dotted your cars up and down the Derwent Valley, walk from one to the other and collect each in turn. Simple. Just take care of the ignition keys.

One of the great truths of hill-walking is that relatives and friends should be scattered all over Britain at strategic points. They will then be handy for the chore of collecting dishevelled, muddy walkers from odd locations which the collectors may previously have regarded as fictional adornments on the Ordnance Survey map. My wife and I had taken the necessary precautions and a tolerant brother-in-law agreed to pick me up. We stayed, however, at the Hathersage Inn – partly because it is a favourite haunt anyway but chiefly because Scotch and Soda, our English and Gordon Setters, cannot be described as unobtrusive house guests. By accident and design in turn, the Hathersage Inn has become accustomed to dogs of all sizes. A few years ago a Border

Collie bitch turned up from nowhere and selected the landlord, David Bowie, as a pet. He calls her Shadow. Having taken over the landlord, Shadow then took over the inn – and now provides package holidays for dogs, with a few titbits thrown in for their retainers. Give the lady ten out of ten for charm and initiative. She is, however, a lazy hostess who leaves all the work to David and the staff. Shadow thinks the staff includes me and, accordingly, has me on the list for such odd jobs as driving her up to the moors and throwing twigs, without respite, so that she can retrieve them. Running an inn is a worrying business, so Shadow has to take a little time off in the cause of fitness and fun.

Shadow lives about two miles off our route and two-thirds of the way along it. Hathersage is a good base and a village of much character and history. Little John, supposedly Robin Hood's lieutenant, was born and buried here. His grave is in the churchyard. One of the vicars was the brother of Charlotte Brontë's friend Ellen Nussey, and in 1845 the novelist spent three productive weeks in Hathersage – productive because they gave her the ideas, the characters and the setting (even the title) for much of *Jane Eyre*. A more mundane item to note is that the local butcher sells tomato-flavoured sausages, which are not readily available in the deprived south.

The English Setter being somewhat arthritic, it was arranged that Soda, the Gordon, would escort me from Slippery Stones as far south as we chose to go without getting into a lather. The morning was promising, sunny but cool, and the drive through Bamford and up Derwent Dale was visually pleasing though historically poignant. Ladybower Reservoir, for example, is beautifully arranged among moorland heights that tempt the walker in every direction. Perhaps the best time to appreciate the scene is at the cocktail hour on an autumn evening, when colouring and lighting harmonise perfectly. The construction work for the reservoir took from 1935 to 1939 and, because of the war, filling did not begin until 1943. The rising waters drowned two villages fondly remembered not only by former residents (rehoused at Yorkshire Bridge, near Bamford) but also by generations of ramblers. The remnants of Ashopton, once known as Cocksbridge, lie under the Sheffield end of the longer of two viaducts. The site of Derwent, about a mile and a half to the north, can be identified if you pause by an oddly isolated war memorial. This stands a little more than a mile along the minor road that branches up Derwent Dale from the A57. If you look across the reservoir towards the wooded inlet at the foot of Mill Brook, you are looking over the submerged ruins of Derwent – from which the war memorial was shifted to its present position.

Just north of Derwent Dam is another memorial stone, facing across the water to moors once well known to the man and the dog whose story is carved on that slab. One of Shadow's breed, a sheepdog bitch called Tip, stayed by the body and eventually the bones of her dead master for fifteen weeks from 12 December 1953 to 27 March 1954 and somehow survived – in spite of the fact that the location, 1,500ft (457m) up on Ridgewalk Moor, is on the edge of Bleaklow. This is a hostile wilderness at the best of times and certainly no place for man or dog in winter. Joseph Tagg, a sheep farmer and dog-trainer of uncommon talent and renown, had retired from Old House Farm, Derwent, to live with his niece at Yorkshire Bridge. With eighty-six birthdays behind him – and a suspicion, perhaps, that there would be no more to come – he told his niece one morning that he had a fancy to visit the site of his childhood home, Ronksley Farm (demolished forty-four years earlier when the Howden Reservoir was filled). It had been the last dwelling at the top of Derwent Dale, where Linch Clough ends its plunge from the moors on which the old shepherd was to die. He was healthy and active and still had some land and a few sheep near Pike Low, east of Derwent Dam. So there was no reason for concern when Tagg and Tip set off from home at 9.30 that Saturday morning. They were last seen plodding up the eastern shore of Derwent Reservoir at 1.20pm.

Tagg had spent all his life in the valley and was widely known and respected. The search was prolonged and thorough. Relatives, friends, farmers, shepherds and gamekeepers were joined by the police, ramblers and the RAF mountain rescue service. What was left of Tagg – plus the wet, weak, emaciated Tip, sleeping a few yards away – was discovered exactly fifteen weeks later by an employee of the Derwent Valley Water Board who was helping to round up sheep. Tip, suffering from malnutrition and long exposure to the wind and snow of a bitter winter, had to be carried part of the way to safety. But she was quickly nursed back to health by Tagg's niece and became an international celebrity because of her extraordinary devotion and its tragic, mysterious circumstances. Yes, mysterious. Man and dog were unfamiliar with Ridgewalk Moor and had no reason to go up there. They must have walked about 14 miles, via Slippery Stones and Ronksley, and Tagg may have been bewildered by the reservoirs, which had drastically changed the landscape vividly recalled from his childhood. The memorial to Tip was erected by public subscription. The headstone on Tagg's grave, in the Roman Catholic churchyard at Bamford, suggests no terminal date. Just December 1953.

There will be an echo of all that, in a moment. But first let us note that Derwent Dam was used by 617 Squadron, the 'Dam Busters', for training in low-level flying over water at night. Farther up the dale, on the north-western shore of Derwent Reservoir, plantations occupy the site of Birchinlee ('Tin Town'), a settlement built to accommodate the labour force needed to construct the Howden and Derwent reservoirs between 1901 and 1911. Birchinlee had about 1,000 inhabitants, including families, and was a self-contained community with all the facilities appropriate to more permanent villages – even a football team. The place was demolished in 1914.

We parked at Ronksley, which was as far as the car could go, and set off along a broad track through a plantation to cross the Derwent at Slippery Stones. The seventeenth-century packhorse bridge here was formerly a familiar sight at Derwent but was carefully dismantled and stored to make way for the Ladybower Reservoir. Nobody was quite sure where to put it or how to meet the cost, and the war intervened anyway. So it was twenty years before the bridge was re-erected 5 miles away and formally opened in 1959. The flagstones came from demolished houses in Sheffield but the rest of the bridge is original. We were just crossing some open ground and making for the eastern skyline when a Land Rover pulled up. Shepherds and dogs tumbled out and we merged into a conversational group while strolling up towards Howden Edge. It was fun to see the collies gambolling about on the moor like puppies before beginning their day's work. We tend to think of them only in terms of hard-eyed concentration and panting effort. Soda was on the lead. He is responsive to commands and behaves well when sheep are about, but I did not want him to do anything daft in the first rush of exuberance after release from the car. The senior shepherd observed with a smile that Gordon Setters were probably a little too heavy for this kind of work anyway. He turned out to be Stuart Ollerenshaw, a family name well known in the Hope Valley and its environs. When I brought up the subject of Joseph Tagg my companion told me he had known the old shepherd and had helped in that fruitless search, almost thirty years earlier. Tagg, he said, was 'a remarkable man' but had reached an age at which he could remember things that happened a long time ago but not always the things that happened yesterday. He had gone back to the haunts of his childhood but probably wasn't quite sure where he was. In short, his memory had played tricks with him. But Ollerenshaw offered no theories about the hints that Tagg's jacket, waistcoat, and boots (which were unlaced) had been taken off; and he thought that at the time of her master's death Tip was too old to hunt and catch anything. In short, there was still a mystery, still scope for guesswork.

We said our farewells but later, on the skyline, I turned to watch the sheepdogs scouring the sweep of moorland around Cranberry Clough. The collies knew their jobs so well that they did not need much bidding. What a delightful spectacle it was, on that clear, sunny morning, to see men and dogs working together with an unfussy ease that, misleadingly, made their arduously difficult craft seem little more than a joyous recreation. We moved out of sight, over the hill, and I freed Soda so that he could stretch his muscles. Gordon Setters are a marvellous sight when responding to the instinctive call of adventure. There is so much strength and bounding energy in them that one suspects a collision with a wall would do the wall almost as much damage as the dog. On Margery Hill (1,791ft or 546m) we reached our first check point: what the Ordnance Survey formally describes as a triangulation station. This one is just a pillar among gritstone boulders on the moor. No sort of peak at all. Merely the highest point on a rather uninteresting lump of the Earth's crust. Strangers to the Peak District should not expect too much from its name, which is a corruption of the Old English 'péac', meaning hill.

We turned south along Wilfrey and Howden Edges. Ahead, there were occasional whistles and shouts. Briefly, Stuart Ollerenshaw popped into view again, working much the same territory as Joseph Tagg used to do. We made a detour to the east, to avoid losing much height, but had to plunge steeply and reluctantly down to Abbey Brook. Reluctantly, because all hill-walkers are aware that at least one cliché can be reversed – what goes down must go up. Before tackling the strenuous second half of this equation I paused beside Abbey Brook for a coffee break. The morning was no longer sunny: instead, grey and dreary, with light rain. It was a pretty spot, though, between two waterfalls. And Soda was inexhaustible in his pursuit of pleasure: dashing up and down the steep slopes, jumping into the brook, drinking, washing, and looking at the day. Suddenly he was motionless, pointing his nose skywards like a War Department sign. On the skyline was a runner, a bizarre figure in such circumstances. It was just some eccentric, perhaps an orienteer (a species prevalent in the Peak District though not peculiar to it). Plodding up the grassy slope on the other side of the brook, I realised that this was going to be a lazy, reflective day. We were soon walking in fog, too. Time was slipping away.

In the vicinity of Back Tor, a compass bearing conflicted with memory and judgement but I believed the compass, which is more reliable. On Back Tor (1,765ft or 538m) there was not only one perceptible path, but several. Beyond the well-known track from Abbey Grange to Strines, we were still in rain and low cloud but caught glimpses of sunny Derwent Dale below us. Ahead was that scattering of rocky outcrops which look, in distant outline, like the experimental doodlings of some half-crazed architect. In the quality and diversity of its immediate and remote views Derwent Edge provides one of the most spectacular panoramas in the Peak District. On this particular day it was a wild, slightly eerie, rather intimate experience because of the shifting vapour. One could not see much – just a suggestion, here and there, that a cloud within a cloud was something more substantial. Vague shapes, mistier and mistier, receded into the distance. The fog thickened. The rain became heavier, drove into our faces, and was briefly replaced by graupel – soft hail. Small birds flitted about among the sandstone boulders and Soda was startled when a grouse took flight with its characteristic rattling noise. The rocky track was crunchy and heather-hemmed. The scenery suddenly assumed a striking disparity. In front of us, enclosing fog blew across our route to the outcrops known as the Coach and Horses or the Wheel Stones, whereas to the west one looked down on Ladybower Reservoir and the greenness of fields and woodland and sunshine and far horizons. Ahead, all was sepulchral. To the west, all was enchantment.

The path was soon crossed by another, pointing in one direction to Moscar and in the other, oddly, to the submerged village of Derwent. We turned towards Moscar but paused for lunch in a shooting butt where the tracks intersected. The rucksack was lighter after I had come to an arrangement with Soda about a can of dog food: he would carry the contents and I would carry the can. Then we walked down the line of neat shooting butts across a hillside of bracken and heather towards the tidily quadrangular Moscar House. Those with a taste for literary history should note that this is probably the area to which the coach brought Charlotte Brontë when she visited Ellen Nussey – and Jane Eyre when she absconded from Thornfield Hall and Mr Rochester in the cause of propriety. The novel is a confusing mixture of fact and fiction, with the characters of authoress and heroine often overlapping. After a brief stretch up the A57 we turned right on the public footpath to Stanage Edge and I had to lift 5st 7lb of Gordon Setter over a stile, an exercise that is by no means addictive. On Stanage Edge we came upon the numbered series of holes carved in gritstone slabs so that the keepers can be sure the grouse always have fresh water (bog water is too acid). Man has some strange ways of leaving his mark on the landscape. Beyond a broken-down shelter was the triangulation pillar on High Neb (1,502ft or 458m). This commands an impressive prospect over and beyond Hathersage, with the escarpment itself extending an inviting arm to the south-east. The scene deserved a contemplative break, so I took a few photographs, escaped the wind by tucking myself in among the rocks for a pipe, and exchanged a smile and a wave with two elderly walkers heading briskly in the opposite direction. Soda gazed intently at two hovering falcons.

As you will have gathered, the weather had cleared by

now and one was therefore amply rewarded for walking in high places. The valley assumed a lusher green as it became more heavily wooded. Stanage is a renowned training school for rock-climbers and after crossing the old packhorse track we met a few aspiring Joe Browns, complete with crash helmets and clanking hardware. Mostly prostrated, they were gazing down at their chums and encouraging the tardy with such terse gentilities as 'Better get a bloody move on, or we shall miss tea'. The next 'trig point', at 1,500ft (457m), rose from a jungle of boulders, and here we swung left in a heavy shower and had a downhill spell past the Cowper Stone, an isolated geological oddity that looks like a vast Rubic Cube stuck on a sloping base. That brought us to Burbage Bridge, a beautiful spot popular with day-trippers from Sheffield. It can be reached by road and commands a view of gritstone heights sheltering the valley of Burbage Brook: a charming diversity of colour and contour. Suppressing a slight sense of guilt, I decided that we should have another break – just to soak in that long familiar scene for old times' sake. Soda seemed to favour the idea, too. So we perched on a rock above the brook and Soda took a nap while I savoured, once again, the extraordinary harmony of colour and light that comes with September and late afternoon. We were closely examined by two sheep, each of which had one horn painted bright red: a rather fetching brand image.

Staying on the tops, as opposed to the Green Drive of childhood memories, we made our way along Burbage Rocks, the valley's eastern rim. To the west were the arresting bulks of Higger Tor and Carl Wark, the latter crowned by the ruins of an ancient hill-fort on a crag that might have been designed for the purpose. I had decided to call it a day at the Fox House Inn, which is inevitably associated with foxes but in fact took its name from a shepherd who built a cottage there in the eighteenth century. We could have pushed on to the designated terminus at Baslow but I did not want to be greedy. The

Limestone pillar on Pen-y-Ghent (*Tom Parker*)

(*above*) Crossing a snowfield on the last lap of the approach to High Cup Nick, Upper Teesdale; (*below*) At High Cup Nick

last lap could wait. So I lifted Soda over a last stile onto the A625 near the Toad's Mouth (a large boulder that looks like a toad squatting by a bend in the road) and strolled up to Fox House. Ignoring the excess of breaks, we had taken seven hours to cover about 16 map miles of mostly easy going on obvious tracks. The wildest stretch had been the highest, from Margery Hill to Back Tor. Partly because of Soda's adventures, the pace had been indolent. Seven hours should suffice, breaks included, for this section from Ronksley to Fox House.

My telephone call interrupted the family dinner at Hathersage and I told my brother-in-law to take his time. After all, the Fox House Inn was open. But I paused on the threshold and asked the landlord if he minded the boots and the dog. 'The dog's all right,' he said, straight-faced, 'but we're not so sure about you.' Moments later he was not so sure about the dog, either, because Soda raised himself to maximum height and slapped his paws on the counter as if impatient to order. Standing eyeball to eyeball with a Gordon Setter is an intimidating experience. Mind you, ten days earlier I had seen a chimpanzee drinking at a bar in New York. She was smartly dressed in pink and behaved perfectly. Her owner sat her on a bar stool, ordered his own drink, and added: 'Orange juice for her. No ice. But she'll need a straw.' And the bartender did not even blink.

The excursion ended with a twilight drive up Derwent Dale to collect the other car. Back at the starting line, as it were, Soda seemed to think we were about to do the whole thing all over again – and clearly relished the prospect. But he was missing when, almost three months later, normal service was resumed. Taking time off from the Hathersage Inn, Shadow replaced him. I was also accompanied by a chum from Darlington, Jeff Todhunter, sports editor of the *Northern Echo*. We always make a point of reporting the British national squash championship. This is played at Abbeydale Park, between Sheffield and the national park boundary, and the press are accommodated at the Hathersage Inn. So Jeff and I pack our boots and find time for a ramble up Burbage or perhaps Win Hill (1,518ft or 463m), which is proudly poised over Ladybower and probably commands the finest panoramic view in the Peak District. Jeff enjoys his walks all the more these days because his active interest in squash and badminton has been terminated by sprains that reduced the lateral flexibility of his ankles.

Anyway, Jeff was game to join me in tidying up the edge walk. So was Shadow. And David Bowie said he would pick us up from the other end if necessary. To tell the truth we were a little pressed for time and therefore missed out the two miles south of Fox House – through the Longshaw estate, a National Trust property well known for its sheepdog trials, and then down the B6054 past the Grouse Inn. Instead we parked at the northern end of Froggatt Edge and, once the doors were open, observed a remarkable transformation in Shadow. She had been curled up on the back seat showing no more animation than a cushion. But at the first whiff of accessible moorland breezes she was like a greyhound coming out of the trap. Then she put us through the twig routine. We took turns, but after an hour or so our arms were ready to drop off. Do not be fooled by that bundle of sleeping Border Collie curled up by the bar at the Hathersage Inn. Given the right circumstances, Shadow can be very tiring company.

The broad sandstone track along Froggatt and Curbar Edges is an airy vantage ground for viewing Middleton Dale, which contains the industrial pother of Stoney Middleton and the better-known village of Eyam, where the plague of 1665–6 killed three out of every four inhabitants. Across Curbar Gap, a dip where the ridge is intersected by a minor road, we paused to look over Curbar. Below us, just before the moor stops at the village, five simple slabs were hidden from view among the heather and bracken. They mark the graves of five earlier plague victims, in 1632. Much closer were two landmarks known as the Eagle Stone and Wellington's Monument. The isolated 14ft (1.2m) Eagle Stone has been smoothly corrugated by nailed boots, and the tradition attached to it demands respect. It seems that the young men of Baslow were not regarded as mature enough for marriage until they had climbed it. The monument, which can be seen for miles, was erected in 1866 by a Baslow man who had served in the Duke of Wellington's Regiment. He did not see why Nelson's Monument, on Birchen Edge across the valley, should hog all the limelight. Historically, though, the star attraction reserved for this last act on our bill was the splendour of Chatsworth Park, spread out before us to the south. The first mansion built there was begun in 1552 and the most distinguished house guest was Mary Queen of Scots, a state prisoner in the custody of the Earl of Shrewsbury. The present palace, as large as a one-piece village, is one of the finest in Europe, and the surrounding woods and parkland – incorporating the same Derwent we first crossed at Slippery Stones – are equally satisfying to the aesthetic senses. Essentially the Peak District is a triumph of nature. But in this particular corner some great artists and craftsmen also did their stuff for posterity.

Jeff and I, still tossing twigs, and Shadow, still fetching them, had to turn back at the Wellington Monument because we had work to do. Baslow is just a mile down the lane. The alternative finish is first to the east (to a crossroads at the confluence of Bar Brook and Blake Brook) and then south across the moor to Birchen Edge, where I learned the rudiments of rock-climbing. This 'optional extra' ends at the Robin Hood Inn and (a mile and a half down the A619) Baslow. If you have a little time to kill, the most interesting area of Baslow is the original settlement of Bridge End, gathered around the church and the Derwent. Note the dial on the church clock, which spells out 'Victoria 1897' (the Queen's diamond jubilee) instead of the usual numbers.

The last and easiest part of the walk, from Fox House

to Baslow, takes about an hour and a half. Add an hour if you digress via Birchen Edge. So the entire route, from the one-time home of Joseph Tagg to the one-time home of Mary Queen of Scots, demands 8½ hours (or 9½). I began it on one clear, sunny morning and ended it on another – having swopped dogs and acquired a companion on the way – and enjoyed every mile. You may, of course, choose to walk from south to north, beginning amid the soft, green prettiness of the Chatsworth area and finishing amid the untamed grandeur of Derwent Dale's eastern heights. It makes little difference. But starting in the north gets the toughest walking out of the way while you are still fresh. Moreover, if there are any transport problems late in the day, they can be solved much more easily at Baslow than at Ronksley. The top end of Derwent Dale is a long walk from anywhere.

Other suggested walks

1 The Pennine Way starts (or finishes) with two alternative routes across Kinder Scout (2,088ft or 636m) and these can be combined in a single walk from Edale – via Upper Booth, Jacob's Ladder, Kinder Low, Kinder Downfall, Crowden Head, and Grindsbrook Clough. Or from Kinder Downfall you can leave the Pennine Way and head for Seal Edge, Blackden Edge, Crookstone Knoll, Crookstone Barn, Jaggers Clough, Nether Booth and Ollerbrook Booth back to Edale.

2 From Castleton there is a choice of approaches to the ancient hill-fort on Mam Tor (1,695ft or 517m) for the ridge walk to Hollins Cross and Lose Hill before descending to Castleton. This short outing would mix easily with a visit to one of Castleton's 'show' caverns.

3 The western flank of the Peak District offers a tough linear route from Lyme Park (near Disley) to the Bow Stones, Sponds Hill, and then across Todd Brook to Windgather Rocks, Cats Tor, Shining Tor, the Cat and Fiddle Inn, Cumberland Brook and Shutlingsloe.

6

Iced Ingleborough

No hill-walker worth his salt can ignore the collective challenge of Yorkshire's Three Peaks. They stand in one of the most attractive and unusual areas of rural England and the task of bagging the lot in one day is an endurance test that demands three separate ascents to summits well over 2,000ft (610m). Whernside, Ingleborough and Pen-y-Ghent have been combined in a single walk since 1887 and some of the hard men who know the route well have come to regard the exercise as a little humdrum. Familiarity does not necessarily breed contempt but it does stale the spice of adventure. Nowadays fell-runners cover the 22 to 24 miles in 2½ hours. But the fact that the walk is so popular and well documented, and has been for almost a century, is evidence enough that it is well worth the effort. And for every walker whose appetite for the Three Peaks is sated, there are hundreds who go back every year to taste, once again, the diversity of pleasures that have taken a firm hold on their affections. Every year, too, there are hundreds for whom the Three Peaks is a new adventure – the most comprehensively satisfying in the entire range of the Pennines.

Those of us who choose to do so can join the Three Peaks of Yorkshire Club – and have a badge to prove it – as long as we touch all three 'trig points', complete the course in less than 12 hours, and then sign in at the Pen-y-Ghent Stores and Café, Horton in Ribblesdale. We can begin anywhere that takes our fancy, but the original route from Ribblehead remains as good as any and has the advantage of getting the highest but least exhilarating mountain out of the way after breakfast. Roughly, the itinerary from the Station Inn goes under the Batty Moss viaduct to Gunner Fleet, Winterscales and Whernside (2,415ft or 736m), then via Bruntscar and the B6255 to Ingleborough (2,372ft or 723m), and finally down Sulber Nick to Horton and Brackenbottom before the ascent of Pen-y-Ghent (2,277ft or 694m) and the return to Ribblehead. All the details and the options are supplied in Arthur Gemmell's footpath map and guide.

The Batty Moss (or Ribblehead) viaduct was in the news at the time this chapter was written. The viaduct needed renovating and British Rail seemed to think that four trains a day did not justify the cost. So they proposed to close the Settle–Carlisle railway (opened in 1876), probably the most spectacular main line in England, and allow the viaduct to become a decaying museum piece. This scheme caused much resentment and led to organised resistance – designed to persuade British Rail to change their minds, or to ensure that the line would have some kind of future under the management of a private company. The construction of the line was an astonishing triumph of Victorian engineering, particularly at Ribblehead and immediately to the north on Blea Moor, where four years of hard labour in appalling conditions produced a tunnel almost a mile and a half long at a grievous cost in lives. The viaduct was begun in 1870 and took four years to build. It has 24 arches and a maximum height of 105ft (32m). To accommodate the labour force for these works, plus their families, a shanty town of wooden dwellings was spread across the bleak moorland of Batty Green. It had a hospital, a library and a post office but was nevertheless a rowdy, lawless settlement where drinking and fighting reached an uncontrollable level in a doom-laden environment. So many navvies had fatal accidents at work and so many more (plus women and children) died from fevers and smallpox that the tally of about 200 premature deaths was too much for the conventional resources of St Leonard's, the squat, grey little church tucked behind trees at Chapel le Dale. The graveyard had to be extended and bodies were buried without the dignity of headstones.

All that was little more than a century ago. Nowadays there is a wild grandeur, a menacing serenity, in the scenery around Batty Green. A man-made giant, the viaduct, challenges the majestic character of the mountains that frame it – Whernside and Ingleborough. The viaduct was only thirteen years old when the earliest Three Peaks walkers devised a route that began up the road at Gearstones, which then had an inn formerly well known to cattle drovers. Even farther back, Iron Age farmers cultivated crops on what has since become bare limestone in the Colt Park area, a mile south-east of Batty Green. During the past 2,000 years or so, soil erosion has considerably extended the limestone 'pavements' prevalent all over the Three Peaks area. These are locally known as clints and the enlarged vertical fissures (many of which provide shelter for rare plants) are called grikes. The Three Peaks are closely related in their composition and height and it is easy to imagine them as a single, connected massif before centuries of weathering scoured out the intervening valleys. The mountains consist of three layers of rock: limestone supporting a band of shale and grit and, on top, a cap of tough millstone grit. Water has not only washed the vegetation from the limestone: it has also created a remarkable assembly of waterfalls, potholes, caves and underground streams. A large area of Yorkshire has thus achieved renown as the Mecca of Britain's potholers and cavers.

Whernside – the name means a hilly source of millstones – is the least exciting mountain of the three, both geologically and aesthetically. Ingleborough and Pen-y-Ghent are more striking because of their steep flanks and flat tops. But whalebacked Whernside, plain though it is, has a long summit ridge that commands wide and impressive views. Should you pass Greensett Tarn, look out for the black-headed gulls. They may have some fun with you. Keith Watson and I cut Whernside from the itinerary because we had to ration our pleasures. His

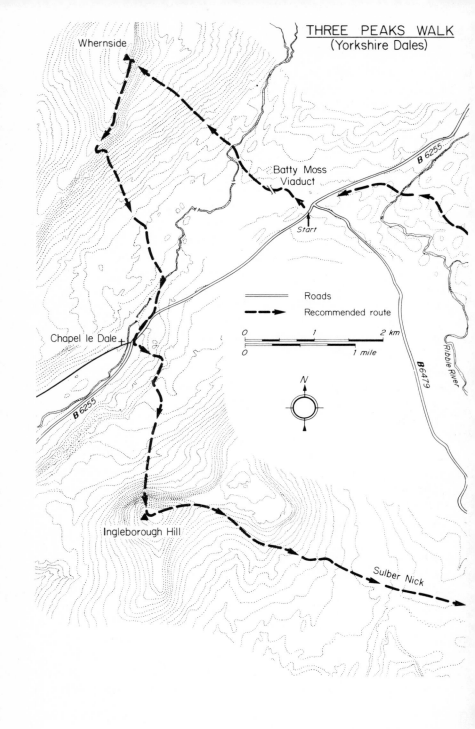

THREE PEAKS WALK
(Yorkshire Dales)

Whernside

Batty Moss
Viaduct

B 6255

Start

Chapel le Dale

Roads

Recommended route

B 6255

0   1   2 km

0   1 mile

N

B 6479

Ribble River

Ingleborough Hill

Sulber Nick

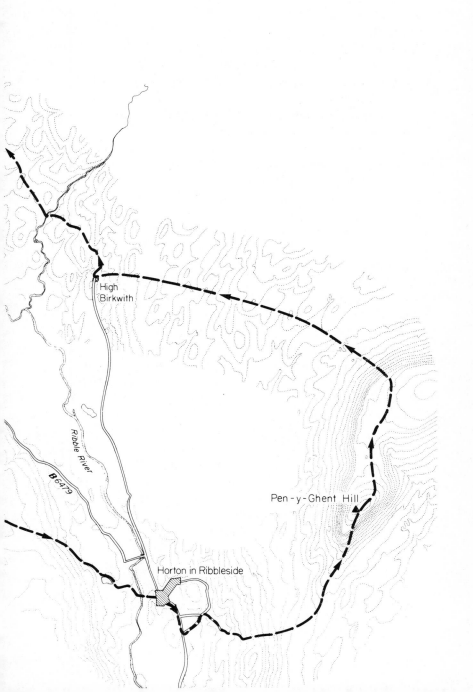

home near Stockton-on-Tees was not the handiest starting point for our examination of the Three Peaks. Moreover, the wintry hours of daylight were restricted, difficult conditions must impose a speed limit, and the terrain was only vaguely familiar. We therefore decided that a chunk or two of the Three Peaks walk was as much as we could reasonably hope to bite off during a short day on tricky going.

Keith is a bearded, gentle, thoughtful man who would look just as much at home in a professorial role as he does on the hills. His quiet passion for the countryside and thorough knowledge of his own patch, the North-East, is condensed into guidebooks and into articles for the *Northern Echo*. In action, he is the most caring and competent of leaders but has one visually puzzling eccentricity: for some reason one sock or the other tends to lose contact with his breeches and descend to ankle level in concertina-like puckers. That is the Watson trademark, the one thing about him that defies his talent for organisation. This particular expedition, though, contained the seeds of a wider disorder in that our common fund of experience had touched only lightly on the Three Peaks. So there was no clear distinction between the leader and the led. We just pooled our judgement and preferences and thus had an easy-going ramble in which a disciplined, driving sense of purpose was only sporadically evident.

We parked outside the Hill Inn, Chapel le Dale, and Keith phoned his wife to tell her that we had reached the starting line and that he did not much like the look of Ingleborough. Prudently, he did not remind her that five days earlier a corpse had been brought down: the frozen body of a hill-walker who had lost contact with his companion while they were retreating from the upper slopes during a 'white-out'. By contrast we had been granted a clear day. There was not much warmth in the sunlight and Ingleborough's casing of snow was ominous. But a blizzard was not even a remote possibility.

Ingleborough ('Hill Barrow') was clothed in white and looked regally formidable. But what an oddly topless sight it is, at any time. There is no peak. It is as if nature had anticipated the Colosseum or the Castel Sant' Angelo but, becoming bored with the job, had left one side unfinished – the lumpy eastern ridge.

We cut across the fields between Ingleborough and its supporting 'pavement'. A fell-runner, doubtless training for something or other, caught and passed us. We watched him with some concern (we were going the same way) because it took him an inordinately long time to negotiate a steep and slippery ascent from Humphry Bottom. That slope turned out to be very interesting indeed. There was ice to deal with before we even reached it, and the wind was bitter. Then came this leaning wall of frozen snow. Kicking steps was at best difficult and strenuous, at worst impossible – and we had no ice axe. We were equipped for walking, not mountaineering. However, there had happened to be a walking stick in the car and as a precaution I had brought it with me. It was useful for seeking out soft spots in the crust of snow and serving as a third 'leg' and an aid to balance. What a nasty climb that was. The treacherous thing about it was that, even where the snow was not frozen hard, it often thinly concealed an icy undercoat. There was always the disconcerting possibility of a slip – the equivalent of an unlucky throw at snakes and ladders. To some extent, this was practice for my forthcoming match (already reported) with the scree slope below Bristly Ridge. Somehow we kicked and clawed our way to the top, often grasping the security of a pig-wire fence. As we admitted later, both of us had fleeting thoughts that, should worsening conditions even slightly increase the hazards, we might have to accept the indignity of retreat. At the summit shelter we met some Army cadets and their instructors, complete with ice axes, and were assured that on such thick, frozen snow it was possible to get off Ingleborough in three minutes by using bums or bellies toboggan-style. We were not in that much of a hurry, we told them. But the refreshment break was not prolonged. We were both shivering with cold, though my six layers of clothing included thermal underwear. The shelter and the view indicator near by were erected by the Ingleton fell rescue team in 1955.

The vast panorama included Morecambe Bay, the Lake District, and our neighbour Pen-y-Ghent: similarly flat on top because, like Ingleborough, it has a horizontal stratum of rock hard enough to resist erosion. Ingleborough's conveniently level summit is notable for the remnants of a fortified settlement stuck up there in the days when the climate was milder and the vegetation more nourishing. It was probably a stronghold of the Brigantes, the hill tribe who dominated the uplands of northern England from the Iron Age onwards and were such a nuisance to the Romans. How bizarre it seems, now, to think of corn growing up there – and enough sheep, goats and cattle to satisfy the needs of that hardy little community. It has been suggested that the Brigantes used Sulber Nick, to the east, as a route to lower settlements in Ribblesdale.

Our own route was south-west, towards Ingleton. It was a relief to escape from the ice and the freezing wind. The extraordinary thing was that we did so within minutes, as if stepping into another world: a Shangri-La. A grassy, peaty, rocky track gave us a sheltered, sunny, easy stroll down Hard Gill ('gill', of Scandinavian origin, means a gorge or deep valley). When Keith observed that we had seen the two faces of Ingleborough, the double meaning was explicit and apt. This side was kid's stuff. On the other hand I would rather go down Hard Gill than up it, which must be rather a tedious slog. We passed the farmstead at Crina Bottom, set among mini-cliffs and the inevitable 'pavements', and met some walkers on the way up. Were they mentally prepared, we wondered, for the ice and the piercingly cold wind they would meet on top? We turned right, across the fields towards Skirwith, a quarrying area. Keith had been breaking in some new boots and they were chafing, so he changed into a lightweight pair in readiness for the trudge up Low Sleights Road by Chapel Beck (a river that changes its name with bewildering indecision, every mile or so).

On the way we passed White Scar Cave, which is on the fringe of Ingleborough's subterranean and aquatic entertainments. There is supposed to be a huge lake under Ingleborough, which could presumably fall into it. The mountain is already extensively cratered and riddled with holes and underground passages, especially on and beneath its southern slopes. The area west of Newby Moss is particularly pock-marked with open potholes and Long Kin (West) is 325ft (99m) deep. But for those seeking side-shows on the way up Ingleborough the most attractive route is from Clapham, almost due south of the summit. A wooded walk up Clapham Beck leads to a show cave, discovered in 1837, that is 650 yards (590m) long and adorned by stalactites and stalagmites. Just to the north is Trow Gill, where human bones found in 1947 were thought to be those of a German spy. Within a few days more bones came to light less than a mile away at that awesome chasm, Gaping Gill, a hole that is 365ft (111m) deep and contains a waterfall with the biggest unbroken drop in Britain: 310ft (94m). The water wanders about underground and eventually finds its way into Clapham Beck. Gaping Gill is on top of the thick shelf of limestone that surrounds and supports Ingleborough. Like Ingleborough Cave and Trow Gill, it is conveniently located on the track from Clapham to the summit.

Breaks included, we took almost 5½ hours over that modest ramble (about 9 map miles), which means that we had not exactly been breaking into a sweat. Nor was there any progress to report in the next hour or so, because although the Hill Inn looked closed it was, in fact, open. More than adequately refreshed, we drove round to Horton. Keith strongly recommended coffee at

the Pen-y-Ghent Café, so it was 4 o'clock before we set off
to discover what Pen-y-Ghent had to say to us. There was
no time to examine the leaning pillars of the local church.
Instead we made our way up Horton Scar Lane, a rocky
track now further embellished by ice, great banks of
snow, and some beautifully delicate icicles. We turned
right at a ruined shooting box, digressing to neither Hull
Pot – 300ft long, 60ft wide, 60ft deep (91m, 18m and
18m), and supposedly a collapsed cavern – nor Hunt Pot,
a fissure with an initial drop of 90ft (27m). All that
concerned us now was Pen-y-Ghent ('The Hill of the
Winds') and the imminence of dusk. Ingleborough and
Pen-y-Ghent are twins: not identical, but very much
alike. The image of an iced layer cake is slightly sharper
in the case of Pen-y-Ghent, perhaps because of the
startling symmetry of the protruding bosses neatly spaced
along its flank like a knotted ribbon around the cake.
When we could see them through the snow we were now
walking on wooden palings laid across the path. This
must be a mucky morass when it is not frozen. The views
to the west were enchanting, with Ingleborough and
Whernside white giants standing on a landscape of tired-
looking greens streaked with grey.

About 200 yards (180m) short of two signposts high on
that spectacular western flank of Pen-y-Ghent, we
decided that prudence must overrule what had in any case
been no more than lukewarm ambition. We had come to
see, not to conquer. And the light was fading. So we
turned back, crunching through the snow and skidding
over the ice and eventually returning to Horton in
moonlight just after 6 o'clock. Thus we missed the full
splendour of Pen-y-Ghent, on which the Pennine Way
(we had walked a little of it) makes use of an old
packhorse track. We missed the ridge walk and the cold
summit, with its surprising hints of primitive mining for
inferior coal. As for the rock-climbs and Pen-y-Ghent Pot
(527ft or 161m deep), we would have missed them
anyway. And it is possible to enjoy the wine without

emptying the bottle. This had been a good day. February, of course, is not the best time of year for the Three Peaks walk as a whole, which insists that one goes up and down three separate mountains. Long hours of daylight are needed and strangers to the area cannot afford the time-consuming handicap of staying on course when every track is covered by snow. It is important to make an early start, at any time of year, and that means finding a bed locally. And when the Three Peaks are wearing white, they are probably best left alone.

Other suggested walks

1 Using much of the accepted Three Peaks route, the two most interesting peaks, Ingleborough and Pen-y-Ghent, can be done from Chapel le Dale (return via High Birkwith, Selside and Colt Park) or from Clapham – via Clapham Lane, Sulber Nick, Horton, Pen-y-Ghent, High Birkwith, Selside, Colt Park and Ingleborough.
2 The two western summits can be combined from Ribblehead House. The route covers Blea Moor, Force Gill, Whernside, Philpin, Ingleborough and Park Fell.
3 Wharfedale offers an alternative airy walk – from Conistone to Mossdale, Great Whernside (actually lower than Whernside), Tor Mere Top, Buckden Pike and Buckden.

7

Teesdale's Pennine Way

The Teesdale section of the Pennine Way is an exciting walk in its own right: always interesting, often spectacular, and also unique in the diversity of natural attractions strung along its length. It contains three acts that, individually, could top the bill almost anywhere else in England. These are High Force and Cauldron Snout, two mighty waterfalls separated by a national nature reserve, and the geological marvel of High Cup Nick, an awesome cliff overlooking a vast glaciated valley. These splendours are so neatly spaced along the route that the dramatic effect of all three is enhanced by the miles between them – rest periods, so to speak, for the aesthetic senses. But those intervening miles are a joy in themselves because of Teesdale's botanical treasury, which most obviously features England's finest forest of junipers, a rare sight these days. The Teesdale traverse also includes one of the highest and loneliest farms in England and may end (if you are unlucky in your timing) with an assault from the notoriously violent Helm Wind. All that, and more, can be packed into one easy-going day that will hardly work up a sweat.

I had an exploratory outing with three natives – Jeff Todhunter and Keith Watson, who have already been introduced, and Brian Hunter, a restlessly active diabetic from Sedgefield. Brian works at a school of nursing and induces hospital employees to roam the countryside under the collective label of the Winterton Wayfarers. He has a special liking for long-distance walks (especially if he can get them sponsored for charitable causes), and is afflicted by what may be a unique talent for falling into holes.

The landowners up there would probably not thank me

for publishing the detailed route of this fact-finding mission. We did no harm but may have digressed from the straight and narrow paths of virtue primly known as public rights of way. Indeed, for much of the day we were bog-trotting, with no paths at all. Moreover, Sod's Law again governed the weather. Sunshine cast a luminous charm over Teesdale's farms and fields and cottages. But there was snow on the ground and up on the tops there was often snow whirling around us. We were even assaulted by stinging hail. And the wind was bitter. It was as if we had left spring behind, in that gentle, peaceful valley, and walked back into winter. Yet the compensations were breathtaking in their beauty and dramatic diversity. The extraordinary thing, throughout that day, was the bizarre, ever-changing cloudscape. There was every conceivable variation of shape, colour, density and light. Nothing was constant. There was no pattern. Mysterious, confusing, totally unpredictable, the clouds rearranged themselves all the time – and simultaneously, of course, rearranged the view. As one curtain fell, another rose. As one spectacle became misty, another became clear. One moment's hint of a far-off, veiled grandeur was the next moment's brightly, whitely swelling mountain. Then it was gone. We could have stayed in one place for an hour and seen a different landscape every minute. Nature never stopped shuffling the pack. Yet behind us, down in Teesdale, all was clear and settled and unchanging. That picture was the work of a conventional artist. In the west, an impressionist had gone berserk.

Boots crunched sharply defined prints into the crisp snow. The wind strengthened as we approached the 2,000ft (610m) contour. Brian fell into a hole (in turn, we all did) but was bubbling over with high spirits and, garrulous humorist that he is, enjoyed baffling the 'foreigner' with verbal salvos couched in the accent and idiom peculiar to the North-East. One of Keith's socks inevitably lost contact with his breeches and came to rest

TEESDALE WALK

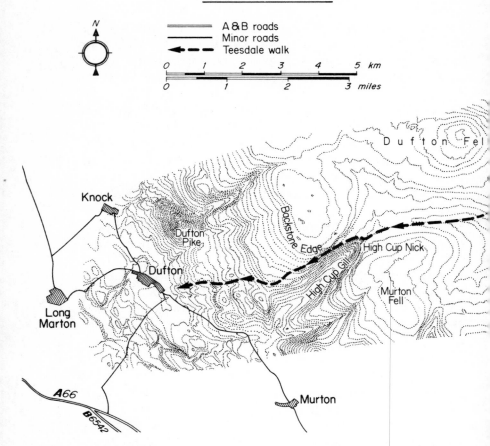

at ankle level. Jeff's genial serenity acquired cause for
mock-indignant wit when a long leg plunged through the
snow and into a pool. At intervals he muttered sardonic
comments to the effect that one foot was sharing a boot
with some very cold water (had he expected it to come out
of the hot tap?).

Our problem, as you have guessed, was the series of
underlying hazards so effectively concealed by the snow.
The bogs and intervening drainage groughs were
unpleasant but familiar enough to be tolerable. The real
villains hidden along our route were those funnel-shaped
depressions, many of them 10 to 15ft (3 to 4.5m) deep, that

106

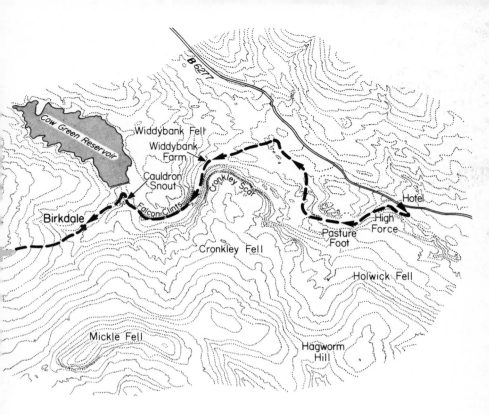

are variously known as swallow-holes ('swallets') or shake-holes. This last expression is prevalent in the area but otherwise unusual. That evening some local men drinking at the same bar told us that 'shack 'oles', as they called them, had been created by a primitive form of opencast mining. This conflicted with opinions later elicited from the Institute of Geological Sciences and one of the most respected authorities on Teesdale's mining history. The definitions seem to be rather subjective and vary with local usage. But swallow-holes and shake-holes are essentially the same: caused by sinking or by the effect of rainwater washing away the soil and boulder clay and penetrating weaknesses in the limestone itself. Several such depressions may occur close together in a straight line – and this applies equally to the shaft-heaps created when lead-miners worked a vein to a limited depth in search of ore that lay close to the surface and could be reached without drilling. In the case of shaft-heaps there should be evidence of excavated material spread over the surface around the hole.

Anyway, all these scattered holes, many containing water, were hidden under the snow. Our progress was therefore irregular, tentative and hilarious. But the compensations were many: not only the distant prospects but, close at hand, such charming sights as prettily ice-encased reeds drooping into a pool. A young man hunting foxes with the help of a double-barrelled shotgun and a Lakeland terrier told us that a bad winter had savagely reduced the population of mountain hares. Scuffing away the snow and using folded over-trousers as waterproof cushions, we lunched in the angle where two walls converged, providing some shelter from the wind. There are circumstances in which the gastronomic observances of polite society cease to be valid. It did not seem unreasonable to wash down a chunk of gingercake with a cup of soup from Keith's flask. 'Oxtail', he explained, as if pampering a fastidious palate. We were soon to have grand views of Mickle Fell, Dufton Fell, Great and Little Dun Fells and Cross Fell, all magnified by the illusion of scale-distorting snow. On Hagworm Hill we met the footpath that links Lunedale and Teesdale. All day there had been hardly a sound except for the angry whisper of the wind but now, suddenly, we came upon Blea Beck, rimmed by snow and icicles. Its laughing waters had such a musical clarity that it was as if someone had opened the door of a room. What a watershed that is: just look at the riot of blue veins on the map. With the escarpment of Holwick Fell to our east, we plunged down to the Tees ('plunged' is not entirely a metaphor), disturbing a few game birds in the heather at Pasture Foot.

The Pennine Way supplied our first visibly genuine footpath for 6 hours. We passed Bleabeck Force and High Force, went through an unusual wooden sheep-gate with sliding bars, and digressed to Holwick Scars to admire the spectacular eastern approach to the Strathmore Estates. Then we clumped down to Middleton-in-Teesdale, doing a few sums on the way. In just over 7 hours, plus about an hour for breaks, we had covered almost 15 miles, a figure offered with some confidence because Brian's accoutrements included a pedometer. In other words we had dealt with some rough and often nasty terrain at the usual unhurried average of 2 miles an hour. The watches also gave us the more immediately relevant and satisfying information that our timing was perfect (or so we thought). We would be among the fleshpots of Middleton at 6.20pm and the inner man could be rewarded for all that pumping up and down. But for all practical purposes Middleton was closed. It seemed deserted, too. Had the place been evacuated? 'It gets late early here,' said Brian, grimly jocular. A mounting sense of disappointment, even grief, was dispelled when we eventually tracked down beer, crisps, pickled eggs, and even, a little later, fish and chips. Simple pleasures, perhaps. But a day on the hills plus beer and fish and chips (as cooked in the North) is no bad formula for contentment.

One way and another that bog-trotting reconnaissance of Teesdale was quite an experience. The banter and shared laughter of companionship had made the expedition a pleasure rather than the penance it could have been as a solo – given the snow and hail, the hidden holes, and a ludicrous spell of wire-walking along a boundary fence that crossed a featureless morass. Next morning, as a loosener before we went to work, Jeff took me to Roseberry Topping (1,051ft or 320m) at the north-western extremity of the Cleveland Hills. This clearly means as much to him as Win Hill in the Peak District does to me. Most of us have these special places, affectionately remembered from way back when. We drove through some pleasant villages and then ambled about 5 miles in 2 hours or so: from the station at Great Ayton (on the single-track Esk Valley line) up to Captain Cook's monument, standing at 1,064ft (324m) on Easby Moor, and down to Gribdale Gate before crossing the edge of Great Ayton Moor to Roseberry Common and the striking mini-mountain of Roseberry Topping. It was a clear, sunny morning and we looked down on the ships at sea outside the Tees estuary. As Jeff pointed out, within 24 hours we had seen the source of the Tees – distantly, on Cross Fell – and then its mouth. The A to Z, if you like, of an attractive area that is very popular among those within easy reach of it but (perhaps because of the absence of sharply impressive peaks) is not as widely known to the nation's hill-walkers as it deserves to be. In this respect Teesdale has much in common with three of its stable-mates in this book: the Peak District, the Cheviots and the Ochil Hills.

All these except the Ochil Hills have, of course, become better known since the Pennine Way was completed in 1965. Keith and Brian, in fact, were in training for the Pennine Way when we had that first trip up Teesdale together. They walked it, too, though I was briefly concerned when two postcards dispatched en route were not succeeded by any triumphal message from the terminus. Had Brian's knack of disappearing into holes become infectious? The Pennine Way must be a remarkably comprehensive test of any hill-walker's fitness, pertinacity and all-round competence at his craft. But the idea of spending a fortnight or so walking from Edale to Scotland is, for me, less inviting than the many alternative means of getting tired. These long-distance walks over set routes can hardly be fun; and when walking ceases to be fun, what is the point of it unless one has something to prove? There is no equation between the duration of an exercise and the pleasure to be derived from doing it. By its nature, rambling is extempore. But that argument cannot be pressed far, because not all hill-walkers are ramblers. And the Pennine Way is a thrilling legacy handed on by all those who, in establishing and connecting so many rights of way, made it possible.

It is possible, moreover, to munch a few apples without going to the trouble of stripping the whole tree. That is what Keith and Brian and I proposed to do when we were reunited almost exactly a year after our first joint foray. Unfortunately Jeff had to work, which meant that at least he was keeping his feet out of cold water. The weather had been appalling and remained ominous. There was so much snow and ice about that it was doubtful whether the Upper Teesdale section of the Pennine Way would, in its entirety, be navigable. But Keith had known the area since he was ten and it was the obvious walk to tackle. In this opinion he had the unreserved support of a colleague of mine on *The Times*, Ronnie Faux, a mountain enthusiast who had lived in Wharfedale for a few years before moving to Temple Sowerby, where he was strategically placed to explore Teesdale in one direction or the Lake District in the other. Ronnie and I shared a room during the Mexico Olympics and briefly dallied with a project we called *The Times* Popocatepetl Expedition. The idea was discarded when research made it clear that this would be difficult and expensive to organise and would take up far more time than we could spare from our professional labours. For all their engaging tolerance of eccentricity our employers would not look kindly, we decided, on two Olympic reporters disappearing up a mountain to contemplate the eternal verities. Anyway, Keith and Ronnie were at one in their respect and affection for Teesdale's contribution to the Pennine Way.

There was no time to find out whether Middleton-in-Teesdale was open or closed. We sped straight through it. Truth to tell, this grey-stone tourists' centre huddled round a green is a pleasant little place to explore during the hours of daylight. A century ago its role was industrial rather than recreational. In 1815 the London Lead

111

Company made it their administrative headquarters for the northern Pennines, but operations were suspended in 1905. The next settlement on our road, Newbiggin, almost died with the lead-mining era. It has an enduring reputation because of the Methodist chapel, in use for more than 200 years, where John Wesley preached. Close at hand are Gibson's Cave and Low Force, both of which repay the attention of Pennine Way walkers who have time for digressive pleasures. Another striking feature of this area, especially when viewed from distant heights, is that the landscape is speckled with whitewashed farmsteads and cottages that are architecturally unusual. Keith, in his booklet 'Walking in Teesdale', refers to two local tales explaining why an annual whitewash is stipulated in the leases. One suggests that a former Lord Barnard, snubbed when he sought a glass of milk at a lonely farm, decided his tenancies should be whitewashed so that he could identify them. The other suggests that when granted overnight shelter he was so grateful that he undertook to foot the bill for repairs to the farm, but was rather put out by the ensuing costs and the discovery that the farm was not part of his estates anyway. Both stories may be true, one reinforcing the other and thus convincing Lord Barnard, the hard way, that there was much to be said for whitewash as an aid to recognition.

We parked on ice outside the High Force Hotel, took a rough track down to the Tees, and walked beside the river to High Force. The morning was a wintry grey, the snow crisply firm. High Force looked even more startling than usual because it was draped with icicles and framed by ice-plastered cliffs. The strange thing about the fall's setting, at any time, is that it is so neatly, almost symmetrically arranged that it might have been sculpted. Many consider High Force to be England's most impressive waterfall. The Tees hurls itself into a gorge 70ft (21m) below with a noise suggesting the simultaneous arrival of several steam trains. Both visually and aurally that mighty fall bruises the senses. It marks the eastern boundary of the Upper Teesdale national nature reserve, which extends to Cauldron Snout in the west. This botanical wonderland, inevitably more enchanting in spring and summer than it is in winter, is remarkable not only for its concentration of floral goodies but also for their unusual nature. Widdybank Fell is particularly well dressed in this respect – as, formerly, was the adjacent terrain submerged by Cow Green Reservoir. The long list of prevalent, flamboyantly named plants reads like a new language invented by a poet. Goodness knows how they came to be assembled in this compact, remote and (perhaps luckily) relatively unfashionable area. A million years ago glaciers shifted arctic and alpine plants into what now seem surprising locations. Or it could be that the green stuff was there already and somehow escaped the devastation of the Ice Age. The prevalence of sugar limestone – coarse and crystalline – has certainly provided a congenial home for plant communities that are throwbacks to prehistoric vegetation.

We squeezed through two constrictive 'kissing gates' and walked along the series of duckboards laid to prevent further erosion of a track that is often waterlogged. There were stretches of boulders and snow-covered ice. On the northern bank were the grey spoil-heaps of a quarry, an unpleasantly incongruous sight in an otherwise wildly natural and attractively peculiar landscape: peculiar because of the vegetation in general and, in particular, the head-high jungle of junipers. The juniper is a native evergreen but seems to be on the way out – in its natural form, that is, as distinct from the trees tamed for our urban pleasure. The Teesdale concentration may be the largest surviving in England. The juniper is a jaunty little tree, a shrub with ambitions. Gin is flavoured with oil distilled from juniper berries, supposedly a stimulating lubricant for the kidneys, and 'gin' is a condensed variant of the Latin, Old French and Dutch words for 'juniper'.

On a rabbit-ridden rise we passed the time of day with a flock of sheep gathered round a corrugated iron hut that bore the painted letters 'PW' and an arrow indicating a right turn for the Pennine Way. Cronkley Fell, to the west, was thinly coated with snow, like an undercoat applied by a parsimonious painter. Ice-encrusted waterfalls seemed to be imitating stalactites, as if some natural upheaval had torn the lid off a cavern and exposed the contents to daylight. The going was heavy and often tentative, because the snow was no longer quite hard enough to bear the weight. We had a delicately icy descent to Cronkley Farm, where a black pony was thoughtfully chewing straw and wondering what to do with the rest of the morning. Suddenly there was a pretty but slightly ominous fall of large snowflakes: ominous because Keith and Brian were well aware of the threat it posed to our flirtation with the 2,000ft (610m) contour on the bare, almost featureless southern flank of Dufton Fell. No matter how well one knows the way, such a crossing has to be out of the question in a 'white-out' at a time when every path and familiar little bump on the landscape is already obscured by snow.

We crossed Saur Hill Bridge (locally spelt 'Sayer'), noting its information for Pennine Way walkers: 'Kirk Yetholm 121 miles, Edale 149'. When Keith and Brian had passed this spot the previous year, Kirk Yetholm had been a destination rather than merely a name on a bridge. Soon we were alongside the Tees again. It was rimmed by huge banks of snow that made the river look like a broad incision in a heavily iced cake. And all the rocks protruding from the water had aureoles of ice coated with snow. Ice and snow. The theme was repetitive. We could not escape it. At Widdybank Farm, tucked in between Cronkley Scar and Widdybank Fell, we took off our boots for a conversational coffee-break in the living room. That isolated farm is the hill-walker's equivalent of the last petrol station before a long stretch of motorway. Even Amber, the Alsatian bitch, seemed to take our arrival for granted, as if some natural law insisted that her privacy should repeatedly be invaded by harmless eccentrics, even during a snowfall on a winter's day. Outside again, we spent a couple of minutes discussing the weather with a mare and foal, noting at the same time that the farm had some uncommon cattle – Kyloes, a relatively modern breed probably descended from semi-wild Scottish stock. Sheep were grazing on Holmwath pastures, overlooked by the frowning cliffs of Cronkley Scar. Except for the livestock, the scene was so bleak and hostile that the imagination was hard pressed to accept the fact that between Cronkley Scar and the Tees were the ruins of a pencil mill, where soft slate was worked to produce pencils locally known as 'Widdies'.

There was some boulder-hopping to be done now. More duckboards. The snow had ceased but the wind was piercing. Bulky icicles, like organ pipes, adorned the dark basaltic crags of Falcon Clints. Small waterfalls, lacking the power to assert their freedom, had been arrested by ice. Cornices of snow overhung the cliffs. Crossing the scree between Falcon Clints and the Tees, we came to the river's confluence with Maize Beck and rounded a right-hand corner. That manoeuvre produced an abrupt introduction to the sight and sound of Cauldron Snout, the longest heavyweight cascade in England. That day the water was a brownish cream. It tumbled and bubbled through a cloud of spray over five falls spanning 200ft (60m). Impressive and intimidating in its own right, Cauldron Snout also has a ghostly legend that presumably grew from a seed of fact planted in the nineteenth century. It is said that a local miner had a girlfriend who was employed at the mine 'shop' to look after the laundry and the cooking and the other domestic chores. When he eventually broke it off, she was so heartbroken that she threw herself into Cauldron Snout. All that is easier to believe than the spooky fancy with which the story has since been embellished. The young lady concerned supposedly haunts the place if the spirit moves her, reappearing to sing mournful ballads when moonlight breaks through the clouds and illuminates

115

those lonely moors. Mind you, anybody wandering around Cauldron Snout on a cloudy night is probably in a state of some mental disorder anyway, and capable of seeing, hearing and believing anything.

On the edge of the fall we took the inevitable photographs accompanied by the inevitable banter: 'Back a bit. Back a bit.' It was time for lunch, too, though we prudently left modest emergency rations in our 'bait' boxes. A scramble up rocks and snow took us to the top of the fall, below the dam of Cow Green Reservoir. Completed in 1970 and officially opened in 1971, the reservoir covers 770 acres. It was created in spite of strong opposition from conservationists, who argued that the botanical splendours of Cow Green were in many ways unique, could not be replaced, and should therefore be cherished rather than drowned. We crossed a footbridge and Keith announced that this was the point of no return, our last chance to retreat. Ahead was the nastiest stretch of the route, across the bare and boggy wilderness of the watershed on the southern heights of Dufton Fell. But there was little cause for apprehension. The weather was now clear and seemed likely to stay that way, and the omnipresent blanket of snow would probably be firm enough to make the going better than usual, rather than worse, over that challenging section of the Pennine Way. This judgement turned out to be sound. The snow was quite deep but mostly solid – and it ironed out the wrinkles.

We soon came to Birkdale Farm, presumably (from the name) a Scandinavian settlement centuries ago. At 1,554ft (474m) it is one of the highest farms in England: and may have been the loneliest until the access routes to Cow Green Reservoir brought civilisation a little closer. Birkdale and the Bainbridges have achieved an inseparable renown. Mary Bainbridge was evacuated from Newcastle to Teesdale in 1941 and, instead of going back, joined the Land Army and married a sheep farmer, Brian. Birkdale had been empty for a year when, in 1952, they moved in – thus restoring to its traditional function a farm that might otherwise have become a deserted and decaying heap of memories, like many more of our once-animated upland settlements. From Birkdale there was a steep pull up to the ruins of Moss Shop. The name sounds a little odd these days. But the word 'shop' originally indicated a crude structure providing temporary shelter. Such refuges were essential for those who worked in lead mines as remote as the one formerly located up here, which could have been the scene of the doomed love affair that gave rise to the legend of Cauldron Snout.

The going had become tough and tiring because, in gaining height, we were breaking through the crust of snow with irritating frequency. The most spectacular breakthrough was achieved, of course, by Brian. Keith was about 100 yards (90m) ahead, sniffing around for the best route, when I heard a startled cry of 'Help!' accompanied by a noise that might be described as a soggy, crunching crash. Brian had excelled himself – plunging through 18 inches or so of snow into a watery, mucky bog. He was immersed to waist level and flailing his arms about in a state of understandable agitation. The spectacle was amusing but its implications were not. I made some sardonic but reassuring comment about his astonishing talent for sudden subsidence. More to the point, I grabbed his arms while they were still available and yanked him out. A week or so later a characteristic note arrived, with a Sedgefield postmark. 'I must thank you', he wrote, 'for helping me out of a hole. It was a very frightening experience, despite my outward panic. I was more afraid, though, of the physical effect it might have in relation to my diabetes. But I must have sorted it out. I made myself a Tandoori chicken dish and no decent germ would come anywhere near that. The dog hasn't been within 10 yards of me for a week.'

For the rest of the walk Brian was a disreputable sight from the waist down. But he had taken his customary plunge – and one of Keith's socks had made its customary descent from the embrace of his breeches. Everything was normal. Gradually losing height, we crossed a huge snowfield, a featureless whiteness that offered not the slightest hint as to what lay beneath it. Brian's curiosity on that subject was satisfied and he was now maintaining a feverishly brisk pace. Maize Beck is notoriously and dangerously violent when in flood but on this occasion was making music and looking pretty. Much of it was hidden under the snow and the visible stretches were decorated with icicles. At ground level, or rather snow level, was the top of a signpost. In tramping over Maize Beck's crisp white blanket, we came unusually close to walking on water. On the other side were two walkers who had come over from Cow Green to High Cup Nick and were on the way back: a double crossing. I waited for Keith and Brian to move ahead so that I could photograph the two figures advancing across a snowfield towards the setting sun and the rim of High Cup Nick. It was a spectacle of chilling beauty.

That waning sun gave us light but not heat. At High Cup Nick we took the full force of a fierce and bitter wind. Thank goodness for thermal underwear. We had to stop for a while, in any case, because High Cup Nick is astonishing – and the third and last of the mighty natural spectacles (the others being High Force and Cauldron Snout) that punctuate this section of the Pennine Way. A great chunk of the Earth's crust has been scooped out so tidily that it looks intentional. To be precise about terms, High Cup Nick – commanding extensive views across the Lake District and the Howgills – is the elevated terminus of a U-shaped valley, High Cup Gill, that was carved out of the landscape by glacial action during the Ice Age. That trench-like gorge is 2 miles long, about 500ft (150m) deep, and is conveniently provided with a natural viewing platform on 80ft (24m) cliffs. It is the combination of the gorge and those abruptly terminal cliffs that makes the scene so breathtaking: plus the fact that the entire horseshoe-shaped depression is so trimly arranged that it

118

might have been a manufactured film set rather than one of the outstanding curiosities bequeathed to us during the making of Britain.

We made our way along the edge of High Cup Gill and down towards the Eden Valley, past the looming bulk of Backstone Edge and the lower but more symmetrical bumps of Dufton Pike and Brownber Hill. That gentle descent should be taken slowly, because the predominantly Lake District panorama to the west is bewildering in its range and diversity. The Pennine Way takes in Dufton, an agreeable offspring of the London Lead Company, and then resumes its route north – towards, most obviously, Cross Fell, at 2,930ft (893m) the highest summit on the Pennines. In addition to its distinctive height and the fact that it is the source of the Tees, Cross Fell is remarkable for furious winds. On its peak the average wind speed is more than twice that in the adjacent valleys. As if that is not intimidating enough, when the wind is in the eastern quarter and whines over the top of Cross Fell, the turbulence in the Eden Valley can be alarming. This is the infamous but fortunately rare 'Helm Wind', which is violent, noisy, attains speeds around 80mph and causes a downward draught strong enough to plaster you over the ground like a mattress.

Our day ended more peacefully than that. For one thing there was the glow of satisfaction: in having completed an exhilarating crossing in hostile conditions without mishap, other than Brian's brief invasion of the underworld. For another, there was the engaging sight of two dogs romping around tractors that were trundling down a hill at the end of the working day. We were in such a sunny mood that six fluffy black horses were forgiven for superciliously ignoring our salutations. Lovely animals, horses – but tricky. Give me dogs any time. Keith had led us flawlessly and his timing was perfect. From High Cup Nick onwards, he had turned a deaf ear to a couple of hints that we might pause for a snifter. He had arranged for a friend with a car and a homing instinct to meet us at Dufton, and was punctiliously aware that such kindness demanded the courtesy of a prompt arrival. Our gallant chauffeur was probably surprised on three counts: first, because we turned up; second, because we turned up early; and third, because when he produced a flask of hot coffee he was offered, in return, a choice of wine or whisky. This last point may have led him to dismiss any lurking suspicions that men who made such a crossing in such conditions must be losing touch with the essential priorities.

We had walked about 16 map miles in 7½ hours, including breaks that added up to more than an hour. This was faster than the usual average of 2 miles an hour – because we had nothing steep or strenuous to negotiate. That evening, Keith took me to his local club for beer and four-handed dominoes. The dominoes expanded my education. So did the words uttered by the amiably authoritative lady who ruled the bar when, near closing time, she noted that my glass was still one-third full (or only two-thirds empty, whichever you prefer). 'Get supping,' she said. I would as soon have argued with Margaret Thatcher. So I supped up.

Other suggested walks

1 A strenuous, day-long walk that begins and ends in the Eden Valley – at Kirkland and Hilton – traverses the summits of Skirwith Fell, Cross Fell, Little Dun Fell, Great Dun Fell, Knock Fell, Meldon Hill, and Mickle Fell before descending Swarth Beck.

2 An easier 'tops' walk is from Dufton over Knock Fell, Great Dun Fell, Little Dun Fell and Cross Fell, then deserting the Pennine Way to return to Milburn via Grumply Hill.

3 As a courtesy, ask the Strathmore Estates if you may do a boomerang walk from Middleton-in-Teesdale: via Kirk Carrion, Harter Fell, Bink Moss, Hagworm Hill, Blea Beck and High Force.

8

Helvellyn and Harrison's Local

The Lake District may be the wettest area in England but, partly because of this unusually effective sprinkling system, it is also the loveliest. The range of goodies on offer is compact yet comprehensive and the beauty takes three basic forms: the expansive grandeur of mountains and lakes, plus all the charming miniatures to be found in valleys and villages. Those valleys are loosely radial, converging on England's highest summits. The mountains are steeper and more spectacular than, for example, those of the Pennines. In addition to all these natural features the Lake District has an uncommonly interesting history – geological, social, racial, literary and the rest. In short, it has something for everybody and consequently inspires admiration, respect and affection – responses that are strengthened, rather than weakened, by increasing familiarity with their sources.

The Langdale crags were reconnoitred and exploited during the Stone Age about 4,000 years ago. They supplied hard rock with a sharp cutting edge. Nowadays such raw material would be shifted to distant, well-equipped factories. In the Stone Age, the axes were made on the spot. The linguistic resources of our neolithic ancestors were presumably limited. But imagine, if you will, that such advice as this must have been commonplace: 'Need a new axe, lad? Pop over to Langdale and ask for Charlie. He'll look after you.' The Lake District has much in common with Norway – most obviously, mountains and water. So it was hardly surprising that in the tenth century, when Norwegian settlers spilled over from their colonies in Ireland, the Isle

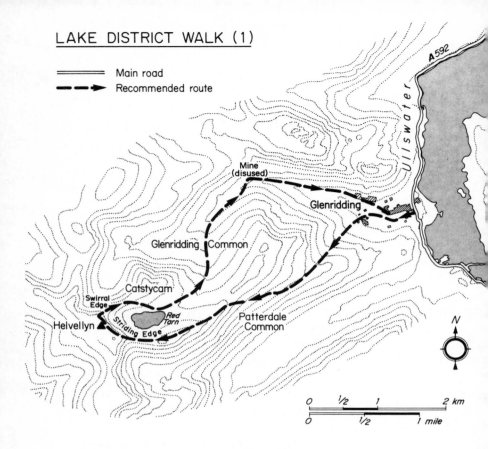

of Man and the Western Isles, they found the Lake District much to their liking. They made themselves at home, probably had a lot to do with clearing the valleys, and certainly made a lasting impression on the vocabulary (and for a long time, the dialect) of the populace. Not only here, but along the northern Pennines, too. Perhaps the best-known examples are 'thwaite' (indicating that a wood had been partly cleared, probably for farming), 'dale' (I will not insult you with a definition), 'fell' (hill or hillside, though its meaning now embraces moorland as well), 'gate' (street or way), 'beck' (mountain stream), and 'force' (waterfall). The Lake District becomes more intelligible, too, if we know that 'cam' or 'rigg' refers to a ridge, 'dodd' to a bare, rounded and often subsidiary summit, 'man' to a summit or the

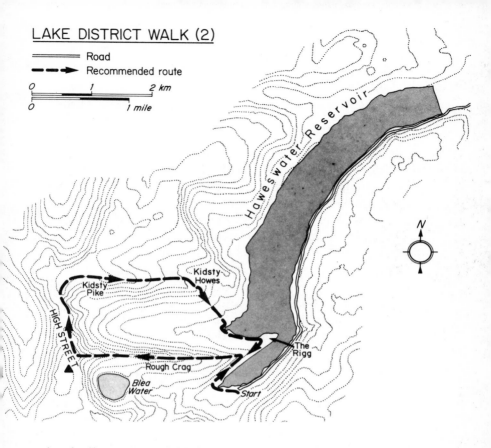

LAKE DISTRICT WALK (2)

Road
Recommended route

0   1   2 km
0   1 mile

Haweswater Reservoir

N

Kidsty Howes
Kidsty Pike
HIGH STREET
The Rigg
Rough Crag
Blea Water
Start

cairn built on it, 'stickle' to a sharp peak, and 'knott' to some rocky protuberance on a hill. Three more words that might reasonably be culled from the local glossary are 'garth' (enclosure), 'keld' (spring), and the prefix 'grise' (wild boar).

Norwegian settlers domesticated the indigenous Herdwicks, hardy sheep born with black or piebald coats that later turn grey. Swaledales, originally from Yorkshire, have a better fleece, are almost as tough as the Herdwicks, and have been a familiar sight in the Lake District since the 1920s. Both breeds have an uncanny knack of finding their way back to the fells where they were reared. This can be a nuisance but, on the other hand, would have given Little Bo-peep a nudge in the right direction. Had her lost sheep been Herdwicks or

Swaledales she would have had a pretty good idea where to find them.

One of the oddest items in the Lake District's occasionally bizarre history was the colony of German miners on Derwent Island, near Keswick. One of their compatriots, an engineer, surveyed the highlands of England and Wales in the sixteenth century and, as a consequence, Germans formed the nucleus of the labour force assembled to develop the Lake District's copper resources – notably in the Keswick area. More familiar and less productive invaders in those days were, of course, the Scots, who had been raiding the Lake District for centuries. The kingdoms were united in 1603 but, as we all know, there was a lot more bother until the second Jacobite rebellion was suppressed. The last battle in England (actually, it was little more than a skirmish) occurred at Clifton, near Penrith, when the Duke of Cumberland's troops set about Bonnie Prince Charlie's retreating army in December 1745.

At that time Thomas Gray, the first of the literary celebrities to popularise the Lake District, was twenty-nine years old and making a name for himself as a poet. Prudently waiting while the dust settled and passions cooled in the Border country, he then toured the Lake District in 1769 and went into print on the subject, thus launching a vogue best remembered for the work of the 'Lake Poets', who were evidently inspired by the peaceful beauty of the environment. William Wordsworth was born locally, at Cockermouth. He went to school at Hawkshead and had a series of homes at Keswick, Grasmere (where he and his sister Dorothy lived in what had formerly been the Dove and Olive Branch Inn), and ultimately Rydal, near Ambleside. Samuel Taylor Coleridge, a chum of Wordsworth's, lived at Keswick for four years, and his son Hartley Coleridge settled at Grasmere. Robert Southey based himself at Keswick. The output of these convergent scribes is striking evidence of the extent to which they lit fires in one

another in what was, in any case, an aesthetically com-
bustible paradise.

Other distinguished writers came and went, adding
fuel to the creative furnace. John Ruskin turned up later
and spent the last twenty-eight years of his life at
Brantwood, which is delightfully located by Coniston
Water – where Donald Campbell was killed in 1967 when
trying to break the world water-speed record. Ruskin was
impressed by medieval craftsmanship and did what he
could to revive it. His experiments included an attempt to
restore Langdale's hand-made linen industry. All these
were writers of exceptional distinction but it must be
doubted if any of them gave more pleasure to more people
than Beatrix Potter did in a very different genre. It was in
a seventeenth-century farmhouse at Sawrey, south-east of
Hawkshead, that she composed and illustrated – with
painstaking delicacy and detail – the imaginative 'Peter
Rabbit' series, which infectiously communicated to
children her well-informed affection for the countryside.

Except for the tourist industry and a few controversial
adjustments to water levels (to satisfy the needs of distant
urban communities), the Lake District remains much as
it was 150 years or so ago when Wordsworth and
company were living there. A 'literary' tour is a joy in
itself. But the purpose of the foregoing notes is to
indicate, in a discursive way, the wider context of our
own modest excursions. These were merely samples. I
had not walked those mountains for many years and
wanted to go back and roam about for a day or two – with
eyes, ears and heart open – and try to catch the
quintessence of the place as it affected one man's sentient
blotting paper during one brief visit.

Keith Watson found time to join me again and rounded
up two mountaineering friends with wide experience of
the Lake District. Keith Harrison, in fact, was living at
Burnbanks and had been for twelve years. He works for
the water authority and Burnbanks was built primarily to
house the men who raised a dam near by – and thus

transformed Haweswater from a natural lake into a reservoir. Our party was completed by Charlie Chapel, a landscape gardener and woodsman who seemed to be inseparable (even indoors) from the unfussy kind of deer-stalker that is known as a 'fore and after' because it looks the same from both directions. Two mountaineers and two hill-walkers seemed a perfect balance as long as Keith Harrison and Charlie suppressed their enthusiasm for challenging the forces of gravity. You know what mountaineers are – show them a slab of upright rock and their fingers and toes start twitching.

The windscreen wipers lay at rest as far as Shap, a lonely one-street village renowned for its tricky weather, for the remnants of Shap Abbey (founded in 1150), and for the little pre-Reformation structure known as Keld Chapel. Shap stands at 850ft (259m). Mist and rain are prevalent. But there must be some magic about the place because it has been inhabited since prehistoric times. My target, though, was down in the valley of the Lowther. Keith Harrison had booked a room for me at his local: the St Patrick's Well Inn at Bampton. This sturdy little pub turned out to be a joy – nothing fancy, but cosily intimate and, in the evenings, very much a social centre for the village. The welcome is old fashioned. Strangers are briefly interviewed by two yellow labradors, Warrior and Shandy, and are then passed on to Alastair and Dorothy Brown (hearty advertisements for the latter's cooking) to be fattened up. I was soon sitting by the parlour fire and savouring a glass of wine and a steak and kidney pie of such proportions that it had to be carefully reconnoitred and outflanked before a frontal assault was practicable. Then the two Keiths and Charlie arrived and we applied internal lubrication while discussing plans for the morrow. It was agreed that Striding Edge and Helvellyn would do for starters. Hackneyed the route may be, but it seemed an ideal 'sample' of the Lake District. There is a hint of perversity in scorning this or that celebrated walk simply because it happens to be popular. True, one needs to explore, to seek adventure, to try a few fancy shots. But professional sport has taught me the consistent importance of the basics in terms of technique and tactics. In the Lake District, Striding Edge and Helvellyn are basics.

The mixed grill served at breakfast imposed a temporary embargo on any form of strenuous exercise. But we had a digestive drive, latterly down the shore of Ullswater past Gowbarrow Park, where Wordsworth had an outing with his sister one day and was moved to write 'Daffodils'. That poem has become as hackneyed as Striding Edge and Helvellyn. But is there another first verse more vividly etched on the memory? We parked at Glenridding and shifted the leg muscles into a low gear for the stroll up to Rattlebeck Cottage: prettily white, though the effect was somewhat marred by an incongruous lamppost in the garden across the lane. The approach to Striding Edge was a steep, slow slog that lifted us about 1,700ft (500m) in little more than a mile, into the inevitable hill fog. It was March and there were patches of snow about. But we could not see far and were already engaged on the Lake District's finest ridge walk before I realised where we were.

From the rocks of Striding Edge the mountain plunges about 200ft (60m) towards Red Tarn to the north and more than three times as much into Nethermost Cove to the south. Obviously it should be exhilarating, as there is not much room for lateral manoeuvres unless one walks on air or uses a path just below the crest – an alternative that is not recommended, as the higher route seemed to me to be more secure and more interesting. That morning we were denied the thrill of the exposure because, except for an occasional hint, the drops were invisible. The problems were merely those of scrambling along a jumble of boulders. Striding Edge can be hazardous in a strong wind, or in icy conditions, and on a clear day the mind must cope with tingling nerves (there is no way of disregarding the depths on either side). But it is by no means as alarming as it looks on most of the photographs or when viewed from the high vantage point of Helvellyn. Even so, Charlie dropped behind for a couple of minutes to act as whipper-in and make sure the hill-walkers could be trusted. Satisfied, he rejoined Keith Harrison and, like puppies at play, they eagerly sought out one or two places that offered modest practice at the finger-and-toe craft. There comes a point when everyone has to do the same thing, because between Striding Edge and Helvellyn is a rocky cleft, a chimney of sorts, that insists on a small dose of rudimentary rock-climbing: trivial, but enough to whet the appetite.

Hereabouts are two monuments that help to concentrate the mind and reinforce one's natural stock of prudence. The first, easy to miss, is on a platform of rock at the end of Striding Edge, overlooking Nethermost Cove. This is the Dixon memorial, dating from 1858, and concerns the death of a pedestrian foxhunter. Near the summit of Helvellyn is a memorial to Charles Gough, whose skeleton – guarded by his dog for three months until a shepherd discovered them – was found there in 1805. This incident, a forerunner of the coincidentally similar story of Joseph Tagg and Tip in Derwent Dale, inspired both Sir Walter Scott and William Wordsworth to put their poetic pens to paper. About 40 yards (36m) south of the cruciform wall-shelter on top of Helvellyn, a tablet set into a cairn marks the spot where a light aircraft landed in 1926. There was no precedent for this sort of thing. Equally extraordinary was the fact that the aircraft took off again. Helvellyn is crowned by a dreary expanse of broken rock with no apparent advantages as a runway. The mountain is deficient, too, in terms of the isolated splendour one might expect from its reputation. It is just the tallest bump on a massive barrier running from north to south between Ullswater and Thirlmere.

The fact remains that Helvellyn is climbed more often than any other mountain in the Lake District. That morning, it was not easy to find enough room within the wall-shelter for four pairs of breeches, and more visitors kept emerging from the fog like spectres. Sipping hot soup and passing round the Valpolicella, I had a fleeting impression that we were sitting on a bench in a busy shopping precinct. But the bustling human traffic can easily be explained. For a start, the 'Hill of Baal' or 'El-Velin' has an air of mystery and in ancient times was supposedly sacred. The word 'Baal' refers to a god and it used to be the custom to light 'Baal' or 'Bale-Fires' on moorland heights on Midsummer Eve. The name Helvellyn has a fine ring to it and the mountain has been given a romantic gloss by the poetry of Scott and Wordsworth. At 3,118ft (950m) it is the third highest summit in the Lake District and England as a whole, behind Scafell Pike (3,210ft or 978m), the home of a rare species of spider, and Scafell (3,162ft or 964m). Moreover, Helvellyn is so accommodating in its location and contours that one does not need to be a superman to get to the top and back and still be too early for afternoon tea. And when the fog takes a day off the views are superb: the Lakeland panorama, of course, plus the northern Pennines and, close at hand, Striding Edge and Red Tarn. Note that Red Tarn, a startling spectacle to come across at 2,350ft (716m), is tucked between the pincer-like heights of Striding Edge and Swirral Edge, narrow ridges created during the Ice Age when the mountain was worn away on both sides.

There were some team changes. At the summit shelter a lad who had lost contact with his party was taken under the collective wing of a group returning to Grasmere. Our own flock now numbered six, because on the way up we had met a Retford couple who were none too sure of the way down to Glenridding. Keith Harrison led us to the exit route down Swirral Edge, which initially looked a little ominous. He pawed the ice-encrusted snow thoughtfully for a moment and then looked around, like a footballer lining up a free-kick. But the thin layer of snow was too soft to be a threat to balanced progress and, lower down, the going soon became more obviously easy. That day we could not see much except for the rocks around us. But Swirral Edge, the north-eastern spur of Helvellyn, is a delightful ridge and one could do with more of it. Catstycam (2,917ft or 889m), which has at least two alternative spellings, lies immediately ahead and – on a clear day – is a temptation well worth the detour. It is gracefully conical, has a genuine peak, and satisfies most of the conventional ideas about what a mountain should look like. Beyond Catstycam, at the top of Glenridding Beck, is a marsh which Nature won back from man. Keppelcove Tarn used to be a reservoir serving the lead mine down Glenridding. In 1927 a cloudburst caused a flood that burst the banks and did a lot of damage, and in 1931 the dam was breached. It was never repaired.

That day, Catstycam was invisible so we left it in peace and descended to Red Tarn, following the beck until its confluence with Glenridding Beck. The heights and the hill fog were now behind us and there was an attractive prospect across the broad undulations of lightly wooded Glenridding. The disused Greenside Mine was a mess of debris that nevertheless inspired mental images of the bustling activity of its heyday: images enhanced by a simple sign identifying the 'bunk house'. By 3.30pm we had said our farewells to the couple from Retford and were browsing around the souvenir shops in the village of Glenridding. Except for that initial, steep ascent to Striding Edge this had been a gentle, lazy day. We had taken almost 4½ hours, excluding breaks, to cover about 9 map miles. Not much more than a loosener but, for all that, a pleasant reunion with the Lake District in congenial company. On the way back to Bampton it struck me that if the shrine of Helvellyn could attract so many pilgrims on 12 March, the mob scrambling along Striding Edge at the height of summer must be in some danger of getting trampled to death or elbowed into space. Keith Harrison said most people set off at about 9.30am and the trick was to start earlier, say 8 o'clock, and thus avoid the rush hours.

That evening the time spent bending our elbows at the St Patrick's Well Inn exceeded the time spent bending our knees on Helvellyn. Thank goodness for Dorothy Brown's liberal interpretation of what constitutes a square meal. This gave us a solid basis for subsequent negotiations with Alastair and his helpers at the bar. He needed all the help he could get. Darts is the big game but on this particular Saturday evening a knock-out dominoes tournament had been organised for the benefit of charity. The place was packed. I suspect the Lowther valley was otherwise depopulated. The sexes were more or less evenly balanced and the age range was the widest permitted by the licensing laws. The congestion was intensified by an unusually high proportion of burly but reassuringly affable men with forearms that might have been sawn off trees. Given such a crowded assembly of arms that might adequately serve many of us as legs, the mind boggled at the demolition that could ensue from a fracas. I estimated that it might take an hour, no more, to transform the pub into a historic ruin. With customers built like that, a dominoes tournament could be regarded as a form of insurance. The only problem, as the brewers' profits mounted, was counting the pips. Keith Watson and Charlie represented us with honour while Keith Harrison and I progressed from round to round in our own way.

It has to be admitted, on the evidence of this sample survey, that mountaineers are more accomplished drinkers than hill-walkers. The hill-walkers eventually retired while still in a condition to find the stairs and circumnavigate Warrior and Shandy without loss of dignity. Keith Harrison and Charlie drank on but told us next morning that they had 'slowed down a bit'. At no time was there the slightest hint that the beer was affecting them. Roy Emerson used to be like that. Perhaps he still is. The most sunny-natured of tennis champions drank a lot of beer but it affected him the way a table tennis ball affects the table. At 3 o'clock

131

one morning, in 1967, I happened to be lying on the
bathroom floor of a friend's house at Boston,
Massachusetts. It had been quite a party. I came to amid
a whirl of flashing lights (in those days 'Emmo' had gold
fillings). He looked down at me and shook his head sadly.
'Jeese, Rex, I'd sure hate to feel the way you look.'
Whereupon he hoisted me over one shoulder like a sack of
potatoes and, some time later, laid the body safely at rest
in a hotel room and went out with some chums to hunt
for an early breakfast.

Keith Harrison and Charlie are the kind of drinking
partners even 'Emmo' would have to respect. Next
morning they were bright-eyed and bushy-tailed and
ready for more exercise. It was Mothering Sunday and,
moreover, Charlie's wedding anniversary was imminent.
But he and Keith Watson arranged an extension of leave
from distant families and Keith Harrison knew just the
walk to fill in a half-day. We parked at the southern end
of Haweswater and stayed in the car for a while because
the weather was better inside than outside. But it was only
a shower and there was no more than the lightest of rain
to bother us as we tackled the mixture of morass, kissing
gates and footbridges that led us around what has, since
1941, been the Mardale extension of Haweswater. That
was the year when the reservoir rose to 96ft (29m) above
the lake's natural level. The village of Mardale, drowned
in the process, was evacuated in 1936. The dam at
Burnbanks was completed in 1940. Manchester's thirst
for water almost doubled the length of Haweswater (now
4 miles) and gave it an average depth of about 135ft
(40m), a figure matched only – in the Lake District, that
is – by Wastwater. Haweswater lies in the kind of
mountainous environment that charms rather than
intimidates. Its beauty was not impaired by the con-
version from lake to reservoir. Merely extended.

On its western shore the path took a Z bend above a
plantation and we climbed steeply, through another brief
shower. For a while there was not much inducement to

break what seemed to be an unspoken agreement amounting to a Sunday morning vow of silence. Such reverent periods of quietude are appropriate to the hills: and convenient, too, when one is breathing heavily. The contemplative calm of our ascent was shattered by the hoarse honking of Canada geese who, down on Haweswater, sounded very angry about something or other. They were introduced from North America for decorative purposes in the seventeenth and eighteenth centuries and are now one of the two species of wild geese common to Britain. They actually breed here. The racket they made shook us all out of our private reveries. We paused and turned to admire the views across the reservoir, and Keith Harrison pointed out the location where what is left of Mardale is immersed in water and memories. The site is most easily identified as the interior of an imaginary triangle drawn from the wooded peninsula of The Rigg across to Hop Gill, on the eastern shore, and the intervening island of Wood Howe.

The story has much in common with that of the Peak District's Ladybower Reservoir and the lost villages of Ashopton and Derwent. But the recorded history of Mardale is in many ways more peculiar. Note, for example, that on the map you will find the word 'fort' near Birks Crag. This marks the place where, on a cliff known as Castle Crag (1,250ft or 381m), the ancient Britons – cute enough to realise that Nature had already done most of the work for them – established a refuge admirably protected from the villainous gangs who used to roam about the Border country upsetting people. You know the sort. Nowadays they would be arrested for disturbing the peace. The Romans and the Scots were prominent among the rowdy itinerants who came to know ˙ Castle Crag. One of the better-known tales, in the days when Mardale still had a community to tell them, concerned a Scottish raiding party who were ambushed by the once-renowned Kendal Archers and buried where they fell: just below Castle Crag.

For 700 years the big noises at Mardale were the Holme family. The founder of this remote rural dynasty, Hugh Holme, arrived there in 1209 in inauspicious circumstances. No peasant, he had estates in Yorkshire but was outlawed by King John and found it expedient to 'tek his hook', as they say up there. He turned up at Mardale, hot-foot, looking for somewhere to hide. A hole in the ground, maybe? Well, yes and no. There was a cave, up Rough Crag. Hugh Holme could not afford to be choosy. As a cave-dweller, he was not living in the manner to which he was accustomed – but at least he was living. He popped out when he dared, and popped back in again when there was the slightest hint of 'baddies' in the area. King John was a nasty piece of work and he and his cronies soon had so many problems that they forgot about Hugh Holme. Safe from pursuit, our hero came out of hiding, married a local girl and settled in Mardale. Socially, he was a cut above the rest of the community and consequently became the local chieftain. The family later built a house near his original cave refuge.

Another celebrity is commemorated at Hugh's Laithes Pike, above the north-eastern shore of Haweswater. Jimmy Lowther was a noisy, foul-mouthed, hard-drinking young rip with a callous enthusiasm for such 'sports' as bull-baiting and cock-fighting. Eventually he hit the bottle once too often and, drunk, broke his neck while steeplechasing. They buried him in the family vault but his restless spirit caused so much alarm in the neigh-bourhood, especially at night, that priests were engaged to exorcise the ghost. They failed. So Jimmy Lowther was dug up, taken to the Naddle Forest skyline, and reburied under an upright stone. This time he rested in peace.

Monks from Shap Abbey had an oratory built at Mardale in 1350. But until 1728, when Mardale acquired a consecrated graveyard of its own, the dead were strapped on horseback and taken over 'The Corpse Road'. You can still walk it. They were carried up Mardale Common to a height of 1,650ft (500m) before the descent to Swindale Head for burial at Swindale – the hamlet is there no more – or Shap. Shepherds used to take their dogs to church with them at Mardale, a practice long extinct when the last service was held there in August 1935. But imagine the busy community of the old days, with flocks of Herdwicks and Swaledales on the fells and, around the valley farms, enough cows to keep Mardale going in milk, butter and cheese. The whitewashed Dun Bull Inn, tucked among trees, was a lively rendezvous for farmers, shepherds, foxhunters and the community as a whole. The beer was distributed in buckets when the shepherds got together. And the sound of laughter and singing echoed down the valley. The Dun Bull Inn and the church and the farms have gone now, except for fading images in the minds of a few elderly people for whom all that was once home. They can remember the look of Mardale, the smell of it, the day-to-day noises of a village that wrapped itself around them – the comforting embrace of a security that was doomed.

Lower down the valley was Measand, once a pre-historic and Norwegian settlement. A grammar school was founded there in 1711. It was only a little school but it gave the children of this remote community a grounding in the classics – and was later to serve as a theological college. Even the road along that western shore of Haweswater has been washed back into history. All we looked down on now (as we made our way along Swine Crag, Heron Crag and Eagle Crag) was the coldly anonymous stillness of water. What graphic names those crags have. The last of them is a reminder that Nature is ever watchful for renewed opportunities. Since the lake was enlarged into a reservoir and Mardale vanished from the landscape, the golden eagle has been seen again around these very heights on which we were walking.

Eagle Crag is not, however, the natural habitat of such earth-bound creatures as dogs and we were therefore surprised when a Corgi suddenly appeared through the mist. Its presence was explained when a couple turned up moments later, but the initial encounter was nevertheless droll. After all, there are dogs and dogs. Corgis may be well known for working with cattle but seem to be a little short in the leg for ridge-walking. At the time we were squatting by a wall, taking a breather and sheltering from a shower. The Corgi gave us no more than a brief, questioning look, just enough to establish the fact that we were dogless and therefore not worth cultivating. Passing occasional outcrops of quartz, we stayed close to the wall until there was no longer a wall. Even on the steepest ground, Keith Harrison walked with hands in pockets, elbows slightly projecting, which meant that from the bum upwards he presented an oddly ovoid outline in the morning mist. South of us was Blea Water, a fine example of the deep basins sometimes scoured out of the mountains by rotating ice. The tarn's impressive depth, more than 200ft (60m), is about half its width. And our route up Riggindale Crag was a reminder of Striding Edge and Swirral Edge, indicating the kind of ridge that was sometimes created when the movement of ice ate into a mountain from both sides.

By this time, though, the hill fog was too thick to permit more than a short-range view of the Lake District's instructive geology. We exchanged mocking banter about the weather but I brought a sparkle to Charlie's eyes with the information that Valpolicella would be served with lunch. This we digested (amid fog, rain, wind and patches of snow) near the 'trig' pillar at 2,719ft (829m) on Racecourse Hill, High Street. It was a situation to shatter anyone's conventional concepts of what constitutes a 'racecourse' and a 'high street'. The broad, level summit of High Street was formerly a rendezvous for shepherds, who gathered there to sort out stray sheep and pass the time of day. This custom developed into an annual fair (it survived until 1835) at which the main event was horse-racing. Thus 'Racecourse Hill'. High Street as a whole was a prehistoric ridgeway converted by the Romans – or,

Conversational pause at Widdybank Farm, Upper Teesdale, with Cronkley Scar in the background

Keith Watson and the author at Cauldron Snout, Upper Teesdale

more accurately, by the slaves who did the dirty work for them – into one of the most remarkable achievements of those obsessive road-makers. The Romans were roaming about the Lake District from roughly AD 80 and, for obvious reasons, had to use considerable ingenuity in planning and laying down the necessary extensions to their network of through routes. After all, they were anticipating John Macadam by more than 1,700 years. One of their roads stretched from Ravenglass, on the Irish Sea, to Eskdale, Hard Knott Pass (where they had a garrison), Wrynose Pass, Little Langdale and Ambleside (another fortified settlement). That took them to the section from Troutbeck over the bare, windswept tops – about 8 miles, most of it over 2,000ft (600m) – to Tirril, south of Penrith, and on to the fort at Brougham (Brocavvm) near the confluence of the Lowther and the Eamont. It was quite an exercise for the imagination to picture High Street as it must have been in Roman days, with all the military traffic and the lumbering caravans of merchants and other travellers. In short, High Street has absorbing associations with prehistory, Romans, shepherds, fairs, and horse-racing. Other than all that – plus the views and the tracks converging from all points of the compass – the rather dreary summit cannot honestly be described as a tourist attraction.

Given his local knowledge, plus such inhibiting factors as the fog and the limited time at our disposal, Keith Harrison decided against the southern route back to Haweswater – via Mardale Ill Bell, Nan Bield Pass (once well known to Scottish invaders), Harter Fell, Adam Set and Gatescarth Pass. Instead we turned north on the Patterdale track but, just short of The Knott (2,423ft or 738m), turned right at a cairn – into the full force of a bitter, stinging wind. From Kidsty Pike (2,560ft or 780m) and Kidsty Howes we plunged steeply out of the fog down to the foot of Riggindale Beck and the ruins of Riggindale Farm. An easy walk back to the car completed an excursion of about 8 miles in less than 3½ hours, plus about half an hour spent on brief breaks. Back in Keith Harrison's house at Burnbanks, those of us with other homes to go to changed into driving gear – with some urgency in the case of Keith Watson and Charlie because, as I said, it was Mothering Sunday and Charlie also had a wedding anniversary next day. They wanted to get back to Darlington and its environs as soon as possible. Alas for good intentions. Many hours later a telephone call conveyed the news that they had broken down at North Stainmore on the A66, which has to be regarded as one of the less desirable areas for a transport crisis. Charlie's wife had to drive over to collect them, which must have put her sense of humour under severe stress. We may assume that, on the way to North Stainmore, she rehearsed a few phrases appropriate to the circumstances.

Other suggested walks

1 A boomerang from Patterdale – via Striding Edge, Helvellyn, Nethermost Pike, Dollywagon Pike, Seat Sandal, Fairfield, Hart Crag and Deepdale.

2 Another boomerang, from Seathwaite, south of Borrowdale – via Sourmilk Gill, Base Brown, Green Gable, Great Gable, Sty Head Pass, Scafell Pike, Scafell, Great End and Sty Head Gill.

3 The Langdale Horseshoe offers several variations but could start and finish at Elterwater, taking in Silver Howe, Stickle Tarn, Langdale Pikes, Stake Pass, Rossett Crag, Bow Fell, Crinkle Crags, Cold Pike, Pike o' Blisco, Side Pike and Lingmoor Fell.

4 Keeping faith with the boomerang principle, start and finish at Hawse End, west of Derwentwater, with intervening mileage via Cat Bells, Maiden Moor, Eel Crags, High Spy, Dale Head, Hindscarth, Robinson, High Snab Bank and Little Town.

5 In the same area is a round trip from Buttermere via Robinson, Dale Head, Honister Pass, Hay Stacks, Scarth Gap, High Crag, High Stile and Red Pike.

6 A pleasant half-day from Braithwaite, west of Keswick, could take you over Causey Pike, Eel Crag and Grisedale Pike.

7 A last boomerang – from Coniston, via Walna Scar Road, Brown Pike, Dow Crag, Brim Fell, Swirl How, Black Sails and Wetherlam.

9

A Cheviot Solo

———◆———

Wooler is an architectural doodle that wanders fitfully across gentle slopes and merges so naturally into the environment that it is as though the little town just happened – growing out of the landscape rather than being imposed on it. A one-street village developed into a busy market centre. Wooler used to be well known for sheep and cattle fairs and until 1251 was also the seat of a barony and had its own castle. Nowadays it keeps pretty much to itself but attracts transients travelling to or from Scotland and has also become a base for the more thoughtful kind of tourists: mainly those with a taste for walking, fishing or history. To the north-west is Flodden Field, where in 1513 the Earl of Surrey's troops beat an invading Scottish army led by James IV – who was killed, as were many of the noblemen serving with him. To the east are Chillingham's wild cattle, unique throwbacks to the prehistoric herds who roamed the Caledonian forests. A small breed with shaggy white coats and black-tipped horns, they contrast rather sharply with modern ideas of what cattle should look like.

Down by the market is the Tankerville Arms Hotel, more than 300 years old. Tradition says it was built to accommodate the overflow of guests at Chillingham Castle. Later it became a busy coaching house on the Edinburgh run. And busy it has remained. The Edinburgh route is still there although the stage-coaches are not; and the Tankerville Arms is so congenially cosy and old fashioned that although the hotel trade is to some extent seasonal, the bar and dining room must always be pleasant rendezvous for those who live locally. The place was certainly lively enough when I turned up on a bleak

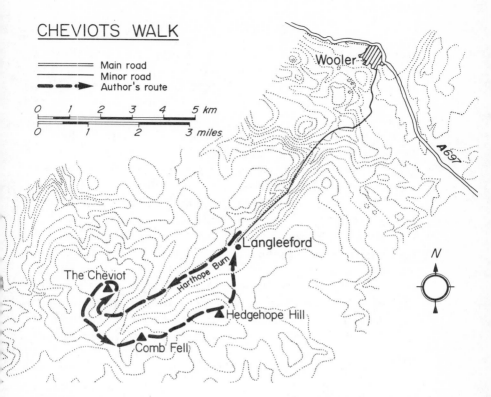

CHEVIOTS WALK

Main road
Minor road
Author's route

0   1   2   3   4   5 km
0   1   2   3 miles

Wooler

A697

Langleeford

Harthope Burn

The Cheviot

Hedgehope Hill

Comb Fell

N

March day. There were two oddities about the first
evening. It was absurd that one should sit in a hotel room
at Wooler typing an article about the way the ambience of
Rome had changed in the past decade. And down in the
bar it seemed equally absurd that lemonade and Pepsi-
Cola should be on tap, whereas the barmaid had to search
some distant corner of the premises in order to produce a
glass of wine. But there was nothing strange about dinner
and, next morning, breakfast: both were so abundantly
tasty that at no time during the day's walk was there the
slightest need for refuelling.

The comprehensive benefits of good food were particularly necessary at the time because the weather
threatened to be arduously exciting. In Wooler's main
street, for example, the wind was strong enough to blow
the bonnet off a car. From the look of them this seemed to
be more startling for the early-morning shoppers than it

143

was for the driver, whose blank face suggested incredulous shock. I wondered what his opening line would be when he introduced car and bonnet, severally, to the local garage. 'Listen. You're not going to believe this, but . . .'

The Border country was temporarily afflicted by fierce, freezing winds and scattered snow. It was sunny enough, but the temperature provoked visions of brass monkeys queueing at the welders. And the short drive along Harthope Burn to Langleeford was visually enlivened by a snowfall subject to such violent air currents that the curtain of whiteness swept by at an angle not far short of the horizontal. The heavily fleeced sheep rimming that narrow, winding, undulating lane looked rather smug. But sheep usually do, in any weather. By a sign that read 'Farm traffic only' there was just enough space to park the car where it would not be in anyone's way. Encased in every available layer of protective clothing I then set off for the hills, telling myself that the combination of scenery, sunshine and wind-blown snow was attractively unusual. This, of course, was tendentious reasoning strongly flavoured by sophistry. Determined to make the best of it, I was kidding myself. Much later, on the tops, it transpired that I was lucky. Walking conditions on The Cheviot can be exasperating because of peat bogs, mud and standing water. The going is much easier when icy weather has hardened the terrain.

The walk up Harthope Burn was agreeable and undemanding: just the thing to summon lungs, heart and muscles to active service and coax them through the post-breakfast resentment of any exertion. This was the first time I had used a tape-recorder on the hills. These little boxes of instant memories are the aural equivalent of the camera, helping us to recapture the immediacy of a scene, a sound or one's momentary reactions. Those first tape-recorded notes, serving as a counterpoint to heavy breathing and the whine of the wind, were understandably terse: 'A powdering of snow. Frozen puddles.

A soft wrapping of low cloud around the tops. The sun veiled.' Yes, that was Harthope Burn as it was one morning in March. This is one of the most delightful valleys in England, because of the harmony between hills and river, bracken and meadow and woodland. Sir Walter Scott, who was then a young man spending much of his spare time exploring the Border country, stayed in the whitewashed farmhouse of Langleeford in the autumn of 1791 and wrote to a friend about the 'simplicity' that resided among the hills.

Upstream from Langleeford I saw a lonely, turquoise-jacketed figure on horseback, slowly climbing a hillside to the south-east. The turquoise seemed out of place in that stern landscape. Three dogs romped around the horse as if urging it along. There were sheep all over the place, huddled together in groups that suggested a punctilious observance of tribal boundaries. They were like football teams having half-time tactical discussions. At Langleeford Hope, the last farm in the glen, the farmer was carrying fodder across a meadow, ambling along with that unhurried gait prevalent among countrymen. Like that figure on horseback, he seemed to be almost suspended in time and space. The scene could have been a Constable landscape.

Even at this low altitude, little more than 800ft (240m), one had to resist the urgent tug of the wind. But the bogs and brooklets were sufficiently frozen to make walking easier than it might have been. Soon I was zigzagging steeply upwards, past deep, crisp, freshly white snow-drifts starkly isolated among contrasting greys and browns and dull greens. Back down Harthope Burn the gently attractive view gained width and distance and subtle changes of colour as it receded towards the horizon. Approaching the burn's source, I reflected how pretty and engaging these mountain streams are – full of fun, chuckling over little falls and around boulders like children at play, and gurgling joyously while they are about it. Thus they bring colour, vitality and music to what is often a rather staid if majestic environment. Higher up, the burn was beautifully dressed in fantastic icicles. I climbed past the scattered wreckage of an aircraft. A riot of mosses. A large snowdrift that induced a second look because, allowing nature a little artistic licence, its outline was a replica of Great Britain's. Going well, I abandoned zigzags in favour of a strenuous head-on assault of what was left of Cairn Hill (2,545ft or 776m), turning occasionally to admire the marvellous panorama – partly white, partly a variety of browns – that was opening up to the south.

That burst of energy shot me onto the summit plateau like a cork coming out of a bottle. And I wandered about for a while, looking for something interesting that might provoke a sense of achievement. True, a 'trig' pillar stuck out like a sore thumb, identifying the 2,674ft (815m) apex of The Cheviot. I explored the subsidiary bumps, sipped coffee for a while in a sandstone shelter, and peered through the inevitable hill fog in search of distant prospects that were occasionally glimpsed but mostly imagined. That morning, the summit of The Cheviot was an awful place. The end of the world. I slipped and lurched across frozen pools and peat hags and lightly scattered snow. The savage wind battered away ceaselessly. And the density of the fog became consistent: visibility 150 yards at the most. The philosopher in me could come up with nothing better than the sporting cliché which insists that the game is more important than the prize. That is probably true of the Cheviot Hills as a whole – pleasant country for the rambler but, at their highest, not particularly striking except for the views available on a clear day. In the hill-walking league they have to be regarded as a second division team.

At the same time it is easy to understand why the Cheviots inspire affection among those who know them well. For a start, they have a violent yet romantic history packed with legendary deeds. The Romans were eventually persuaded, the hard way, that this part of the island was best left to people they regarded as barbarians. Then came centuries of Border warfare between England and Scotland. The bloodshed was still going on, sporadically, when Daniel Defoe climbed to the boggy summit of The Cheviot – and was still vivid in the memory when Sir Walter Scott made the same ascent. The basic character of the Cheviots owes much to the fickle, windy weather that must always be expected on hills close to the sea. The Cheviots are prominent for their bulk rather than their height: which is to say that their conformation is that of hills rather than mountains. They are not notably grand or rugged but, in less evident ways, have the wild aura of mountains – space, solitude and an almost-silence. The contours are mostly steep but smoothly grassy, the summits broadly bare, the glens often deep and narrow and lonely. Sheep farming is big business. The prevalent breeds are the grey-faced, hornless Cheviot and the hollow-cheeked Blackface. That all adds up to give the Cheviots a distinctive quality that has been far more widely appreciated since Kirk Yetholm, a few miles north-west of the summit, became the terminus or starting-point of the Pennine Way.

Given better weather and more hours of daylight, I would have gone over the top to return via Hen Hole and College Valley. Hen Hole is a rocky chasm in the western flank of The Cheviot. A burn dashes and tumbles down a gorge that captures the spirit and the awesome beauty of the Border country at its best. Perhaps lazily, I decided to leave Hen Hole for another day and, instead, improvise a route back to Langleeford via the other side of the Harthope valley. During the descent through that ghostly half-world in which claustrophobic hill fog gradually gives way to longer and wider views, there was a sudden movement – so startling in that desolate, misty and eerie setting that for a moment it chilled the blood. Just a brief, quick movement. Then nothing. I was motionless, nerve-ends twitching. But the black-tipped ears gave it away: *Lepus timidus*, better known as the 'mountain' or 'blue' hare. Its coat changes colour in spring and autumn, providing natural camouflage. When the brown of summer mixes with the whitish hue of winter the coat temporarily has a bluish tinge. The sample in front of me merged almost imperceptibly into the grey-white background. For a moment it was as still as a stone. Then it vanished – so fast that it was hardly a memory.

Wind and fog gave way to quietness and clarity – and even, in the distance, a patch of sunlight. Until such winds stop, one does not realise how persistently noisy they can be. Across the head of the valley I tramped through heather and slid and stumbled up and down peat groughs. Up Comb Fell (2,133ft or 650m) there was a path, the first for hours. There was also boggy ground and a layer of snow, and Sod's Law decreed that as I moved up, the clouds moved down. A grouse fled, with the usual startling cackle. The next and last hump of the day was Hedgehope Hill (2,342ft or 714m), where a mess of sandstone near the triangulation pillar offered shelter enough to justify another coffee break. Then I plunged steeply downhill, jarring ankles and knees and associated muscles, and used some fancy footwork to cross the burn onto the track trodden earlier in the day. Cows were bellowing. Other than the music of water, the soughing of the wind and the hoarse laughter of a grouse, I had heard no other sound all day. As for signs of life, as distinct from sounds, there had been only a figure on horseback, three dogs, sheep, a farmer, a hare and a grouse. Both aurally and visually, this had been one of those lonely days in the hills that refresh the soul. At Langleeford there were Blackfaces and some handsome cattle that I could not identify. And as if in obeisance to some natural insistence on symmetry, the day ended as it had begun – in sunshine and wind-driven snow. All that remained was to look after the outer and inner man with a hot bath, dinner and a carafe of wine at the Tankerville Arms.

This walk covered about 12 miles in 5 hours, plus a total of 45 minutes or so devoted to coffee and contemplation. During the drive back to Wooler I felt a twinge of regret that I had not attempted more. On the other hand, it is always wise to have some energy and daylight in reserve, especially when roaming solo over desolate and unfamiliar terrain in tricky weather. Twice it had been prudent to take compass bearings. But the hills can be enjoyed in all seasons and one substantial plus mark on this particular day was the firmly frozen going on notoriously mucky tops. Granted another free day within reach of the Cheviots, I shall certainly walk those tops again. And it should be noted that they are an ideal loosener for anyone on the way to the more rugged challenges of Scotland.

Other suggested walks

1 As has already been indicated, there is an attractive variant of the route described here. From Langleeford and The Cheviot, go west down to Hen Hole and the College Valley, which offers a choice of possibilities for returning to Langleeford or Wooler.

2 A boomerang from Cocklawfoot (south-west of The Cheviot) takes you south-east to the cairned Pennine Way, between Windy Gyle and King's Seat, and then up The Cheviot – returning via Hen Hole and Auchope Rig.

10

Fitness Test: the Ochil Hills

The Ochil Hills – the name comes from the Celtic 'uchil', meaning high ground – have inspired many poets. They may be small in relation to Scotland's better-known heights, but there is a compensating beauty in the smoothly grassy slopes, the burns and wooded glens, and the ambience of lonely serenity. Like the Cheviots, they could be an anticlimax after any excursion to the wild, rugged mountains of northern Scotland. The Ochils are charming rather than challenging. But they provide a delightful loosener for anyone on the way north, are easy to reach because of the network of roads around them, and give much pleasure to the considerable local population. They lie between Perth and Stirling and this in itself must be a strong recommendation for anyone with a sense of history and the time to indulge it. Part of that history remains tangible in Castle Campbell, which is attractively poised, near Dollar, on the popular approach to the Ochils. Those friendly hills and intervening glens are also so typical of Scottish scenery that they demand the attention of any Sassenach engaged in what the pollsters would call a sample survey.

For the author the Ochils were ideal for another purpose. A strained Achilles tendon had enforced ten weeks of abstinence from strenuous exercise. By that time it was August, the sun was shining, and a great truth dawned: the bumps on Scotland's landscape had clearly been designed by Nature for the rehabilitation of any Achilles tendon that happened to be under suspicion. It could be nursed back to health with due care. I would drive and walk on alternate days and thus explore three different areas in a week without doing anything to

150

OCHIL HILLS WALK

Main roads
Recommended route

0   1   2   3 km

0   1   2 miles

A 823

Innerdownie

Glenquey Reservoir

Tarmangie Hill

Whitewisp Hill

King's Seat Hill

Castle Campbell

Dollar Glen

Dollar

A 91

N

Tillicoultry

A 91

Start here

contravene the precautionary principles governing convalescents. This exercise in basic philosophy put the author in the same school as two far more distinguished students of high places. C. E. Montague, under doctor's orders to avoid violent exercise for a month, interpreted this injunction as permission to go rock-climbing in Wales – an experience that inspired his dazzling essay, 'In Hanging Garden Gully'. And consider the case of the Everest mountaineer, Frank Smythe. When invalided out of the RAF and advised to avoid exertion (and take care when climbing stairs), he went to the Alps and clambered up the Aiguille du Plan and Mont Blanc – by the Brenva route.

By comparison, my own plans were mere coddling. The only difficulty lay in selecting three walks from the multitude available in a land that is a paradise for hill-walkers or, for that matter, mountaineers. An easy start was necessary, just enough to shake off the rust of inactivity. Then one could be a little more ambitious. As convenient a trio as any, it seemed, would be the Ochil Hills, the Five Sisters of Kintail, and finally whatever took my fancy in the vicinity of Loch Assynt. I decided to go alone, partly because it would have been selfish to ask anyone to take a week off at short notice, and partly because a companion's pleasures could be ruined if that Achilles tendon let me down. But my wife had a bright idea. Why not take our strongest, most agile dog – Soda, the Gordon Setter? Why not, indeed. He was boisterous, fearless and in eight years we had found no way of slowing him down. Perhaps a concentrated dose of hill-walking might do it. He would certainly not funk anything asked of him.

You previously met Soda in the Peak District, but the walks in this book were undertaken as and when each was convenient, rather than in the tidier sequence in which they are printed. Until he invaded Scotland, Soda's frenetic pursuits of free-ranging pleasure had seldom lasted more than half an hour. He knew little about the hills and was totally unfamiliar with the perils of gadding about on rocks above steep drops. But that 5st 7lb of Gordon Setter was and is a natural survivor – and a good companion. He would need careful surveillance, though, when there were sheep or other livestock about. And his presence would deter me from voluntarily tackling any finger-and-toe work on the rocks. Dogs are not rock-climbers. There were two further points to remember. Too much dashing about on rocky ground can tear a dog's pads. And a frisky dog covers about three times as much ground as a man: which means that a dog must be leashed, or made to heel, if he shows any tendency to burn up his energy too soon at the beginning of a long day on the hills.

This question of companionship is interesting. The loneliness of high, wild country is part of its charm: an essential part, too. Most of us find it a refreshing contrast with the busy communities in which we earn our livings. We appreciate people all the more by occasionally getting away from them. During a solo one is imaginatively sensitive to all the sights and sounds and smells of the hills – and has total freedom in choosing a route and following it at one's own pace. But the solo is recommended only for those experienced in hill-craft, because if anything goes wrong – twisting an ankle, getting lost, or whatever – there is no help at hand and eventually a rescue team may have to be assembled. Most of us prefer to share our pleasures – and on the hills it is safer that way. Hill-walkers are a reflective but congenial breed and (as demonstrated during several of the walks described in this book) almost any casual combination can achieve a relaxed, unfussy rapport and have a good day together. Some people are happiest in crowds: and large, organised parties can be fun, in addition to educating the inexperienced in the lore of the hills or providing a guided introduction to unfamiliar terrain. Children, like dogs, demand special care and consideration. As a rough criterion, children can walk as many miles as they have years. They want to stop more often than we do, in order to satisfy some intense if passing curiosity about this or that.

Walks of exceptional merit are savoured to the full only if they are done at least twice – once in company, because the pleasures are shared and the responses more varied, and once alone, because the senses are then more acutely and exclusively alert to the environment. In preparing these essays I went to several unfamiliar or half-forgotten areas and, through force of circumstances, walked alone or with Soda, or with friends old or new – in numbers ranging from one to eleven. For all their diversity, in terms of companionship every expedition was rewarding in one way or another. Four may be the ideal. Such a compact group (a suitable car-load) allows scope for the conversational variety of shifting pairings without loss of unity – and at the end of the day four is the most convenient number when sitting in the bar-room or at the dining table.

On this occasion everything was new. I had done no serious hill-walking in Scotland, was going to three unfamiliar districts, and for the first time was taking a dog on the tops. Even the terminus of the first long drive was in some doubt until, having drawn a blank at Dollar, we booked in at the Bridge Hotel, Tillicoultry. The inn was simple but had everything we needed. That evening, Soda was so full of beans that he would have reduced the bar-room to chaos but for the fact that he was safely tethered.

Next morning we were on the road at 8 o'clock. Tillicoultry, well known in the sixteenth century for its production of serge, now looked tired and grey. So did the small groups of early-morning people – patient, quiet, introspective – who were waiting for the blue and cream Midland Scottish buses. We walked up to Dollar, a village snugly gathered around a longitudinal green following the course of a burn. The well-known academy was founded by a local boy who went into shipping and prospered. The name Dollar may be connected, as the currency is, with the German 'thaler'. This refers to a valley. Silver mined in a valley was made into coins which developed into a standard unit of currency known as 'thalers'. Thus, eventually, 'dollars'.

Dollar Glen is like a doll's house – its features are all reduced in size, condensed into a neatly compact form. In this case the features are natural except for the steep board-walks. The glen winds and climbs past pretty little falls and in places is so leafy that it is almost cavernous. Soda was non-stop, racing this way and that with

154

Striding Edge from Helvellyn, Lake District (*Tom Parker*)

(*above*) In Glenridding, during the descent from Helvellyn; (*below*) Soda, rock-jumping hero of the Five Sisters

uninhibited joy. The glen was a new and exciting adventure and he was reluctant to leave any part of it unexplored. The glen belongs to the National Trust. So does its obvious terminus, Castle Campbell, once the seat and stronghold of the Argylls. The Scots are dramatic raconteurs with a style all their own, especially when describing the dark deeds of their history. On such occasions they go in for protracted vowel sounds and much lugubrious head-shaking. Mournful monologues are milked for all they are worth. It is all done with such practised Thespian skills that sensitive listeners can be afflicted by spine-chilling nervous reactions. How rewarding it could be to wind up one of the better-informed natives on the subject of Castle Campbell and its legends. The castle lies between the Burn of Sorrow and the Burn of Care and itself was known as Castle Gloom until the Earl of Argyll changed the name in 1489. If you have tears, prepare to shed them here. The present structure was begun in the 1480s, burned by Cromwell's troops about 1654, and later restored. The main feature is the north-eastern tower.

The sturdy, grey little castle stands on a knoll among larger, grander hills. The setting is additionally spectacular because of the surrounding woodland, the contorted landscape, and the wide views over and beyond Dollar and the valley of the Devon. Behind the castle, swelling heights climb into the hill fog. They did that morning, anyway, and I briefly questioned the wisdom of roaming the tops on this random basis – a day here, a day there, making hardly any concessions to the weather. Walking the hills is exhilarating at any time but walking the actual tops in poor visibility can be futile: except for the exercise, the practice in compass work, and the satisfaction of overcoming a challenge. The sensible thing to do, perhaps, is to stay in one place for a week or so, adapting one's daily explorations to the weather. But that is not the purpose of this book. We are not making a meal of anything; just enjoying a wine-tasting.

I paused for a chat with a man painting a gate, his head cocked to one side like an artist assessing the effect of every brush-stroke. We walked through a plantation along a broad, grassy, occasionally stony track rimmed by conifers and heather and bracken. It occurred to me, as I looked around, that a basic knowledge of botany opens windows in the minds of all hill-walkers. The wind gently toyed with a wide range of musical possibilities. But it was one of those quiet mornings on which the senses are acutely aware of the secret noises and quick movements of birds among vegetation and foliage. For an hour Soda had been bursting with excited energy, as if he could not believe his luck but was determined to make the most of it. Then he took a breather: standing still occasionally, sniffing the air and looking around thoughtfully. But Soda does not spend much time in neutral. He is convinced that life must be lived in top gear.

So far there had been no sheep except for a few at Dollar, on the golf course across the glen. But there were tufts of wool along the path we were following towards Glenquey Reservoir, so I leashed Soda in readiness. He had met sheep before, but not often, and there was no knowing what he would have to say to them. The first we saw were posing on a bluff high above us, etched against the skyline like Red Indians in a Western movie. As we moved down the glen the sheep moved round the bluff so that they could watch us all the way. Others were scattered around adjacent slopes, but not close enough to provoke Soda to more than an impassive curiosity. Soon there were more, gathered on and alongside our path, and I kept up a soothing monologue to Soda as we walked through the middle of them. He was interested and alert (as they were) but never tugged at the lead. No problem.

By the shore of the reservoir I stopped for coffee and a pipe, sticking the spent matches deeply into the soil. Soda sat alongside, looking this way and that, listening to the sheep, the birds and the burns, and possibly wondering why the mist was overhead instead of in the valley below, as it is at home. He was visibly thinking, trying to work it all out. After all that racing about in water and vegetation he was, by this time, a mess. We show neither of the dogs. But Soda once won a tail-wagging competition while we were on holiday in Devon. The only other competitor refused to get off his bum, which meant that there was no way his tail could budge – no contest. But the blue ribbon – we still have it – says nothing about that. Simply 'Chivenor Festival, 1977. First'. Soda was now gazing so intently at a single sheep, grazing 100 yards away, that it came as quite a shock when he realised that two more were scrutinising him from 25 yards behind his back. His paws shifted restlessly as they moved in and circled around us, reversing the usual roles. Put it all down to the further education of Soda.

Diverting though it was to see the way Soda reacted to the hills, the sheep and all the rest, the real purpose of our expedition was to have an exploratory ramble on the Ochil Hills and find out if that Achilles tendon could take it. The idea was to go up Innerdownie (2,005ft or 611m) and then walk over to Whitewisp Hill (2,110ft or 643m) and across the head of the Burn of Sorrow to King's Seat Hill (2,126ft or 648m). After that I would balance what was left of the day against what was left of my energies. It was a modest enough scheme but did not quite work out – partly because of Soda and partly because of the hill fog.

The first task was to climb an estimated 1,000ft (300m) or so in roughly three-quarters of a mile, up the grassy, tussocky flank of Innerdownie. We soon rose above sheep level. There were still one or two about but, as he comes to heel quickly, it seemed safe to let Soda off the lead. That was daft. Indefensible. Because dogs are unpredictable and in gaining height we moved into hill fog that cut visibility to about 50 yards and wrapped us in clammy silence. Even the bird noises had receded. The going was steep, strenuous and slow. I was taking compass bearings and simultaneously keeping Soda in sight. We spent about 40 minutes gaining height, and must have been near the top when our soundless progress was disturbed by some stray bird. The sudden clamour was startling – and Soda pursued its source at top speed, back down the hill through the fog. Reluctant to concede even a yard of hard-won height, I stood there for a while, calling him in. No response. This was worrying. A loose dog roaming about unfamiliar country in fog made no sense at all. There was nothing for it but to go back, the way we had come up, and hope that – once out of the fog – I would spot a villain dressed in black and tan. He was lying a few yards from the site of our earlier break by the reservoir but had his back to me and, when summoned, did not even turn his head. You know how it is with children and dogs when they feel guilty. They look the other way and go stone-deaf.

After all that wasted exertion I was soaked in sweat and rather vexed. A few well-chosen words were addressed to Soda and on the other side of the reservoir a lonely angler looked up with interest. At the back of my mind, though, was the thought that perhaps Soda had more sense than his handler. Was it unreasonable to prefer this pleasant environment, with its wide views and lulling rural noises, to the vapourish upper slopes where we had been cut off from all the sights and sounds of the countryside?

An hour after the coffee break we were having lunch in the same place. I lit another pipe and reconsidered the afternoon programme while the villain lay beside me and looked at the day. Innerdownie could remain a bad memory. But Whitewisp Hill was worth a shot. So we retraced our steps along the glen for a while and then turned up a delightful burn, a sparkling musical medley of frisky little falls and rippling pools. I soon had bog-trotter's boot – there was wet mud in it. Soda was in and out of the burn for a while and then decided to go straight up it, which simplified his navigating until he discovered a pool deeper than he was. Then we were in the fog again, amid the gathering quietness of the hills and the bones of long-dead sheep. The ridge between Innerdownie and Whitewisp Hill was a damp, grassy wilderness. The silence was broken by an eerie, almost human coughing sound. The cause was distasteful: Soda was vomiting. He had exercised too strenuously on a full stomach. Moreover, this was the greatest adventure of his life and he was excited. On our later walks he showed more discretion because he knew the form.

Instead of traversing across to Tarmangie Hill (2,116ft or 645m) and the head of the Burn of Sorrow, which would have been rather pointless in the absence of a view, we followed a fence steeply down towards our route of the morning. This was turning out to be rather a haphazard ramble. But if the way ahead is invisible it is no bad idea to improvise an alternative. This line of thought is a reminder that the walks we may find in formal guidebooks, stating the distance covered and the approximate time needed, assume that one either knows the route or at least has a clear sight of it. The distance and the time both increase when one has to navigate over unfamiliar terrain in fog. On this occasion the change of plans was not particularly frustrating. After all, the three purposes of the walk were all being served: I was getting to know the Ochil Hills, testing a tendon, and giving Soda a basic education in hill-craft.

The view soon extended for miles rather than yards. Castle Campbell was in the picture again as we plunged down that rocky hillside amid bracken and the five-pronged, pale mauve harebells (Scottish bluebells). Down in the glen the weather was clear and warm, but the encircling tops were still hidden behind grey curtains. Retracing our steps through the plantation, we passed the time of day with two couples and a dog. Behind Castle Campbell there is a wooden footbridge over the burn and we took a break there. Soda ate a few biscuits to replace the lunch he had lost in the clouds. It was a Monday afternoon, the beginning of a local holiday, and a procession of visitors were strolling up the glen from

Castle Campbell. They joked about Soda's wet, dishevelled appearance – a consequence, primarily, of his direct method of ascending burns. But at least he was clean and calm. Tired too. Hardly raising his head at the sight of children and dogs, he settled down for a snooze. That had no part in the immediate programme but I let him get on with it while I sipped sherry (in the absence of 4 o'clock tea), admired the scenery, and chatted with the children attracted by the spectacle of a quiescent Gordon Setter. The Burn of Sorrow looked impressive: a deep, wooded cleft almost buried among the hills. Another hill-walker arrived – easily distinguished from the rest by his breeches, boots and rucksack and balanced, economical gait. Have you noticed how, in the cause of balance, hill-walkers and mountaineers and shepherds tend to have a little more air between the knees than is customary? We talked of the futility of walking the tops on such a day. He had local knowledge and had been up King's Seat Hill, he said, only because he knew the way. For our return trip to Tillicoultry he recommended either of two routes, and as we had already been out for nine hours I chose the most direct. It was strenuous, though, because we wandered off course.

From Castle Campbell a charming ravine leads up the Burn of Sorrow. Pestered by the flies of late afternoon, we then climbed a rocky gully to the shoulder between King's Seat Hill and Bank Hill (1,129ft or 344m). On the southern slopes there were wide views of the Devon valley. Even Soda paused to admire the prospect. I savoured the magical restorative qualities of an orange – food and drink in one compact package. A jungle of bracken was tough going, because it was taller than me and left Soda in the dark. There was not much running in him now. He padded along behind me because there was nowhere else he wanted to go. Sheep-proof wiring at dog level forced me to lift him over two stiles, which was no easy task. It seemed that at this weary stage of our expedition he rather liked the idea of being carried. We were both very tired over the last stretch through Tillicoultry to the Bridge Hotel. In the bar they hardly recognised the boisterous Gordon Setter of the previous evening. Soda had a dish of water and then collapsed in a corner, oblivious to everybody and everything. Later he tottered slowly upstairs, stiff-legged.

For different reasons – I was out of condition and Soda had never tackled such a walk before – it had been an exhausting day for both of us. Excluding all the breaks for this and that, we had been on the move for almost 8½ hours and had covered about 17 map miles. On the telephone that evening I told my wife that although the information had no practicable application to our normal domestic routine, I had found out how to reduce the irrepressibly energetic Soda to a gently heaving heap of fatigue. All it needed was 8½ hours on the hills.

Other suggested walks

1 All the main tops can be incorporated in one long but rewarding day – from Dollar to Castle Campbell and Glen Quey, then up to Innerdownie, Whitewisp Hill, Tarmangie Hill, King's Seat Hill, The Law, Ben Cleuch, Ben Ever, Blairdenon Hill, and finally down Glen Tye to Dunblane.

2 The above walk can be shortened at either end: by going from Castle Campbell up the Burn of Sorrow to King's Seat Hill (thus cutting out the Glen Quey section) or by returning from The Law or Ben Ever to the A91 and the railway path to Dollar.

3 The Ochils can be traversed from south to north (Tillicoultry to Blackford) via the Upper Glendevon Reservoir and Glen Bee. This walk can begin with Daiglen Burn and Ben Cleuch, or with Gannel Burn and King's Seat Hill.

11

Soda meets the Sisters

———◆———

Any discussion about the most exhilarating ridge walks in the British Isles could easily boil down to a comparison between the awesome barriers that reach into the clouds north and south of Glen Shiel. Both must also be high on the list of priorities for the breed known as Munro-baggers. In 1891 Sir Hugh Munro, an original member of the Scottish Mountaineering Club, tabulated all the Scottish mountains over 3,000ft (914m). There are 276. He tried to climb the lot and almost made it. But in 1919 his progress was terminally checked by death. His name lives on because Scottish peaks over 3,000ft became collectively known as Munros and always will be. Among hill-walkers the weight of tradition must remain, in this respect, a stronger influence than the metric system. Munro-bagging has inevitably become a popular subsidiary incentive for anyone specialising in Scottish peaks – and if we may borrow a metaphor from cricket, Glen Shiel, with its short boundaries, is just the place for scoring some quick runs. The north ridge spans about 10 miles, the south ridge about 8. Either can be traversed the long and hard way from the Cluanie Inn and this east-to-west route is also recommended for piecemeal exploration, because the views of mountains, lochs and sea happen to be better in that direction. The North Glen Shiel Ridge incorporates the classic crossing of the Five Sisters of Kintail: Sgurr na Ciste Duibhe (3,370ft or 1,027m), Sgurr na Carnach (3,287ft or 1,002m), Sgurr Fhuaran (3,505ft or 1,068m), Sgurr nan Saighead (3,048ft or 929m) and Sgurr na Moraich (2,870ft or 875m). 'Sgurr' indicates a sharp peak. It was on these Five Sisters that Soda and I, both refreshed by a day of

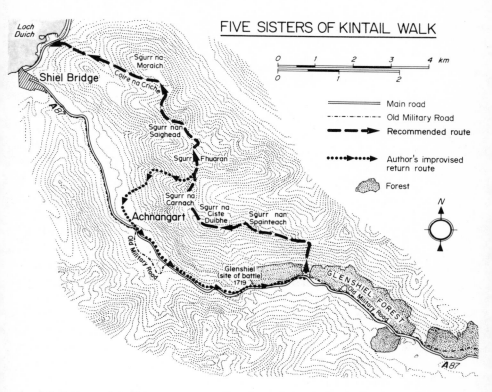

Loch
Duich

Shiel Bridge

A87

Sgurr na
Moraich

Coire na Criche

Sgurr nan
Saighead

Sgurr Fhuaran

Sgurr na
Carnach

Achnangart

Sgurr na
Ciste
Duibhe

Sgurr nan
Spainteach

Old Military Road

Glenshiel
(site of battle)
1719

GLENSHIEL FOREST
Old Military Road

A87

| 0 | 1 | 2 | 3 | 4 km |
| 0 | 1 | | 2 | |

Main road
Old Military Road
Recommended route

Author's improvised
return route

Forest

N

driving and idling, now concentrated our attention.

The obvious place to book in was Kintail Lodge, a former shooting lodge perched between the Five Sisters and Loch Duich on the road to Skye. The receptionist scored a plus mark within seconds by pointing out that, should Soda need it, there was a dog blanket in the top of the wardrobe. A hotel that not only welcomes dogs but provides for their comfort is definitely worth patronising. Life would hardly be tolerable without children and dogs around us. The first half of that equation turned up later that evening after we had dined well and had a stroll by the loch. In the sitting room an American of each sex, neither of them into their teens, engaged me in a long and earnest conversation about dogs in general and Gordon Setters in particular. Though the dining room was rather gloomy and the bar rather remote, Kintail Lodge was otherwise so comfortably congenial that it was popped

165

into the address book for future reference. Be warned that next morning (it was a Friday and some 'readies' were needed, to see me through the weekend) I had to cash a cheque there because the nearest conventional source, Dornie's mobile bank at the other end of the loch, opened only in the afternoon. There are areas of Scotland where such facilities as hotels, banks and petrol stations are thin on the ground.

We parked a mile east of the spot where, in a setting of rugged grandeur, the Battle of Glen Shiel was fought in June 1719. This fracas demands notice because it impinges in so many ways on the doings of any visitor with his mind in gear. Several political pots were on the boil at the time. The Act of Union had forged a fragile bond between England and Scotland. The Treaty of Utrecht had transferred Gibraltar from Spain to Britain. The Hanoverians had become Britain's royal house. The Spaniards were cross and so were the Jacobites, who thought James II ('Jacobus' in Latin) and his descendants should have the throne. So Spain sent some troops to reinforce a Jacobite rising. They came up Loch Alsh and occupied Eilean Donan Castle, at the confluence of Loch Alsh, Loch Long and Loch Duich. Then came this scrap in Glen Shiel, where the Hanoverian redcoats sorted out the combined forces of the Jacobites and Spaniards. Research suggests there were about 1,500 troops on each side. So the glen must have been disagreeably crowded – and noisy, too, with all the echoes bouncing off those mountainous ridges to north and south.

The English then decided to do something destructive about Eilean Donan Castle, because they were fed up with the place. Its inhabitants, Jacobite sympathisers, had been a nuisance for far too long. In that same year, 1719, three men-of-war were sent up Loch Alsh and blasted most of the castle off its rocky island. Nothing was done about the ruins for 200 years. But in the 1920s and 1930s Eilean Donan Castle was rebuilt (much as it had been) at enormous expense. Linked to the shore by a bridge and causeway, it has since become one of the most photographed showpieces of the Scottish Highlands and gives much pleasure to tourists. It became a stronghold in the thirteenth century and is primarily associated with the Mackenzies (later the earls of Seaforth) and the Macraes. But we must beware of over-romanticising Eilean Donan Castle. Much of its early history was associated with organised villainy.

It would be perverse to close the mind to the story of Eilean Donan Castle and the Battle of Glen Shiel. And it would be equally perverse to ignore the remarkable consequences of all that excitement in 1719. The series of Scottish rebellions earned General George Wade, the MP for Bath, a place in history that might otherwise have eluded him. In 1724 he was sent to Scotland to look around and report back to the government with his recommendations as to what should be done to pacify and civilise the country. He was appointed commander-in-chief for Scotland and in 1726 began to construct a network of military roads which were also used by drovers. This explains the words 'old military road' that appear on the map of Glen Shiel and elsewhere. The general employed about 500 soldiers. They received sixpence a day in extra pay and he jokingly called them 'highwaymen'. Roads and bridges added up to an impressive feat of civil engineering that, within three years, considerably improved communications between remote Scotland and the rest of Britain. Meantime England's military presence in Scotland was increased and the Highland clans were disarmed – with such unfussy cunning that they hardly knew it was happening.

That 'old military road' along Glen Shiel has now been replaced by the busy A87. There is a convenient parking area near a gap between two sections of Glenshiel Forest. On getting out of the car, one immediately confronts a steep, grassy climb up the gap. The angle of the winding, rather vague path is a bit much at a time when the taste of coffee and marmalade is still fresh on the palate. But the terrain might have been flat for all the effect it had on Soda's exuberant, head-on assault. Up ahead were a party of five, the only people we saw on the ridge all day. I climbed slowly but gained height quickly, pausing occasionally to look down on our point of departure.

From above, one notes that in briefly swinging away from each other, road and river create a neatly elongated diamond or lozenge shape between them. It was raining lightly and within 50 minutes of leaving the car we were in the clouds. They drifted this way and that, in and out among the hills, permitting no more than tantalising glimpses of the glen and, beyond it, the South Glen Shiel Ridge. The belts of cloud were always shifting, so there was no clear pattern to anything. The effect was rather like that reconnaissance of Upper Teesdale except that now the clouds were more mischievously playful.

Rudimentary cairns mark the upper section of the path. At 2,400ft (730m) the bealach or beallach (pass) at the top is the lowest point of the North Glen Shiel Ridge. For a few moments there was nothing to be seen but the rocks, grass and heather in front of our noses. Then those teasing clouds parted to expose a superb prospect of the mountains gathered around Gleann Lichd and, close at hand, the path we had to follow along our own ridge. The vision was sudden, startling. Soda did a slightly alarmed double-take as a peak shot out of the thinning vapour beside us like a diver coming up for air. The break at the bealach was brief because it was obviously a good idea to keep moving and gain height while we could see where we were going. The rocky, grassy path was easy to follow, but walking that ridge was nevertheless exciting and somewhat eerie. The clouds were drifting to and fro, rising, falling, curling – like steam from a kettle that was standing in a draught. On either side of the ridge the clouds were so close – about 50 to 100 yards (45 to 90m) below us, blotting out all downward views – that we seemed to be walking on air, or on the fuselage of an aircraft frozen in flight. The track had no visible means of support. There was an odd, thrilling sense of being totally isolated at some indeterminate point between the Earth and the troposphere.

Soda was now leashed and gave me a tug uphill – which was only fair because, after all, I was carrying his lunch and water. The proximity of boots and paws sometimes demanded fancy footwork. Ahead of us, the long ridge curved gently up into the sky and vanished into emptiness. Occasionally Soda stopped and looked down at the clouds, as if wondering where the rest of the world had gone to. We traversed Sgurr nan Spainteach (3,248ft or 990m), which took its name from those Spaniards who fought at the Battle of Glen Shiel. The ridge now consisted of large, jumbled rocks – easy scrambling for me but genuine rock-climbing (his first taste of it) for Soda. He often paused but never flinched, and always came on when summoned. Twice he had to jump into my arms because the drop was too much for him. He knew it was too much, but was puzzled rather than frightened. He would have taken the entire plunge if necessary, but the consequences could have been damaging for him and tricky for me. The idea of getting down from a mountain with a Gordon Setter wrapped round my shoulders was not inviting. So I scrambled down those short pitches and then turned, held out my arms, and called 'Come!'. And Soda, trusting and brave, never even hesitated before dropping the few feet between us.

The ridge bends to the north between Ciste Duibhe and Carnach. For the third time, almost vertical rock forced me to bear the weight of an armful of Gordon Setter. I gave Soda a piece of Kendal mint cake and told him, frankly, that he was doing a great job. There was more rain and the clouds closed in again. On Carnach, visibility was down to 20 yards or so. Dimly, two spectral figures appeared on a rock. A voice announced: 'It's the man with the dog.' We were walking through the middle of the party who had been ahead of us on the first climb from Glen Shiel. They had become separated – in thick fog, on top of a mountain. Somebody deserved a kick up the backside. With a mixture of sympathy and disapproval I offered to stay put for a while, as a rendezvous point within hailing distance, while the strays were rounded up. Then they were off again, while I consulted Soda and the map and compass and realised that a 10.40 start from the car had been indiscreetly late. We descended to a mini-ridge between the wide glen of Allt a' Choire Dhomdain ('allt' means stream and the more usual 'coire' refers to a steep-sided valley) and some nameless cleft in the landscape to the west. We were shortly to know the latter a good deal better and if it needs a name I can offer a wide choice, none of them fit for family reading. In losing height we had gained a view, a beauty too. The main belt of hill fog was above us. At this lower level there was no more than a thin vapour, like the smoke from a garden fire but without the stench.

We were scrambling steeply through the fog again, up the rocky slopes of Fhuaran (the biggest of the Five Sisters), when a wave of tiredness confirmed that I no longer had the strength to give Soda the help he sometimes needed – and might continue to need. On the mountains, fatigue is often a symptom of hunger. That problem could easily be solved. But this time it seemed that food alone would not be an adequate restorative. The Ochil Hills had been useful in terms of general conditioning after a long lay-off from exercise. But I was not yet fit enough to endure the broken rhythm of sustained rock work without feeling the effects. Moreover, it must have been thirty years since I had done any hill-walking on such rugged terrain as this (the Glyders expedition was to come later). What with all this, and the strong-arm stuff with Soda, the lassitude was hardly surprising. The Five Sisters traverse is not difficult. Nor is it particularly strenuous for the normal run of hill-walkers. But in the circumstances pertaining to this one man on this one day, the work-load was a little too much. The Five Sisters had been stimulating company. Now I was round about the 3,400ft (1,030m) contour, could not see the way ahead, and no longer had the energy to advance Soda's education in scrambling. The evidence all pointed in the same direction: down. In view of what happened later it might have been wiser to eat and rest, complete the planned route to Loch Duich, and get a lift back to the car. But there was no way of knowing what would happen later. So I decided to retreat to that mini-ridge between the two valleys, have some lunch, and – with the help of the compass – improvise a descent almost due west into Glen Shiel.

The efficient use of map and compass can iron the wrinkles out of a day on the hills by keeping us pointed in the right direction whatever the weather – and may even represent the difference between life and death. The only way to become familiar with these navigational aids is by regular practice, preferably under expert supervision. But the inexperienced may welcome a few hints. Ordnance Survey maps are packed with information: not merely the maps themselves, but also the explanatory notes and symbols on covers, corners and margins. By carefully studying the map of an unfamiliar area it is possible to devise a route and list all the identifying features (both natural and man-made), plus all the ups and downs. Then we can test our map-reading competence by actually doing the walk. The knack of visualising the terrain by advance study of a detailed map is not all that difficult to acquire.

We need a compass, too, for reference and reassurance – and in poor visibility the compass is essential. The lines from top to bottom of a map run more or less from true north to true south. Magnetic north varies but at present is about 6 degrees west of true north. This means that when the compass settles it will point about 6 degrees west of those vertical lines on the map. Spread out the map, put the compass on it, and turn the map until the compass needle points 6 degrees west of the true north indicated on the map. That done, the map is set – and the features on the map correspond, directionally, with those around us. We usually know where we are. By locating our position on the map and using a pencil or something of the sort to link it with the next objective, we establish the line of advance. All we have to do then is look up, from the extremity of that line, and follow its imaginary extension over the terrain ahead of us. On that imaginary extension there will be some natural feature that can serve as a target. In fog, it is necessary to improvise. Ask your companions to walk ahead. Keep them on the required line until they are almost out of sight. Then join them – and do it all again. This is a tedious, painstaking business but it can keep us out of trouble. In poor visibility the navigator should be at the back of the party, ensuring that they stay on the correct bearing.

The circumstances are more interesting when we do not know where we are (which is inexcusable) in thick fog. We can sit it out for a while, waiting for the weather to clear, or we can descend with care until it is possible to see something. There may be fleeting indications of natural features identifiable on the map. Allowing for magnetic variation, we take an instant compass bearing and draw the appropriate line on the map. Then we do the same thing with a second feature, preferably at right angles to the first. There are thus two lines on the map and they intersect – exactly where we are standing. Complicated? Not really. It just needs practice. In my teens I sometimes headed for an unfamiliar but safe corner of the Peak District and deliberately got lost. This was a good way of getting to know the area – and of learning how to use the map and compass. Never forget the necessary allowance for magnetic variation. In some places (the Cuillins, for example) the rock itself is magnetic and we can therefore forget about the compass. It goes crazy.

Most of us are familiar with two simple tricks that give us a rough bearing on those occasions when, improvidently, we forget to pack a compass. Deducting an hour

Hedgehope Hill from The Cheviot (*Leonard and Marjorie Gayton*)

Castle Campbell, Dollar Glen (Ochil Hills) (*Scottish Tourist Board*)

in summer time, we point the hour hand of the watch at the sun, assuming it is visible. An imaginary line bisecting the angle between the hour hand and the figure 12 points south. And, again deducting an hour in summer time, we can be reasonably sure that the sun will be east at 6am, south-east at 9am, south at noon, south-west at 3pm, and west at 6pm. If you go on the hills with neither compass nor watch, then there is nothing to be done for you.

Streams are mostly born in soggy but otherwise harmless terrain and there is a common misconception that following a stream downwards is a useful way to get out of trouble. On some of our gentler hills that may be true. On the mountains it is a sure way of getting into trouble rather than out of it. Consider that streams grow larger as they lose height, and for thousands of years have been washing away the vegetation and getting down to bare rock in deep gullies. They take big drops in their strides. They go where you and I cannot. Consciously flirting with just such a hazard, I decided to make use of the easier upper section of my chosen ravine and, at some well-chosen moment, traverse out of it onto the more open slopes to the south. But the moment was not, in this instance, well chosen. The error of judgement doubtless arose from a combination of tiredness and, for many years, inexperience of this sort of caper. There was also some simple rock-climbing to be done and I enjoyed this so much that pleasure overruled discretion.

First, though, we descended from Fhuaran and found a suitable spot on the ridge for a restful lunch. I rummaged about for the over-trousers and stretched them out on the grass. Just room for two. Soda lay down and, as was becoming his custom, flung a paw casually over one of my boots before he relaxed for a nap. In an unfamiliar world, he needed the reassurance of contact. We were the same age, relatively, and both appreciated the break. It was a long time since I had done so much scrambling about on rocks, and Soda had hardly done any. But he had been agile, sure-footed and confident. He was going very well indeed. By this time there was very little water left in the plastic container. Water is heavy to carry and must be drunk sparingly because, on the tops, there is seldom a chance to top up. Mist was swirling around us but, lower down, the day was clear. I estimated that the 'short cut' back to the car would cover about 6 map miles: assuming that the rugged and rocky mountain permitted us to stay on the compass bearing, we should have wheels under us in 3 hours or so. In fact, the difficulties were such that the trip took 4 hours and 20 minutes.

At first all went well. We heard the strange but welcome sound of water running underground, which meant that the dehydration problem would soon be solved. A little, steep-sided gully dropped rather quickly but we could see a long way down it, to the point where the clouds below blotted out the view. Unfortunately progress was barred by an impassable waterfall flanked by cliffs as close to the vertical as made no difference. Definitely a 'no-go' situation. So I filled up the water-bottle and retreated to cast around for an alternative means of descent. This turned out to be strenuous, but fun. Two sharply angled slabs of rock had to be negotiated. They amounted to no more than modest exercises in the finger-and-toe craft. For Soda it was a different story. Those slabs were so deep that, had I clambered to the bottom and called him, one of two things would have happened: he would have demurred, or he would have flattened me. And he could not be carried, because I could not get down without using my hands on such holds as were available. Some intermediate lodgement was necessary, so that Soda could slither into my embrace before gaining irresistible momentum, and then slither over the second half of the course on his own.

Such lodgements were available. Even so, the ensuing spectacles would have done justice to a circus act. It must be doubted whether Soda saw the ludicrous humour of those rapid drops over very little. Perhaps he did. What

176

happened was that I climbed halfway down and found holds for the toe of each boot and the fingers of one hand. Then I called Soda and, when he arrived like a bomb, grabbed his collar with my spare hand before he shot past to the rocky, grassy ground beneath us. Thus decelerated and congratulated, he returned to all fours and – there being no ledge on which to linger – peformed a skidding solo to the bottom. The hazards were not excessive. It must be doubted if either slab was more than 35ft (about 10m) and they were by no means vertical. Even so, these manoeuvres were asking too much of Soda. Dogs should not be involved in such gymnastics. Amusing though the incidents were, they rammed home the obvious truth that even the fittest, most agile and bravest of dogs are not equipped for rock-climbing. They can scramble but they cannot climb. That must be remembered when planning routes.

Farther down the ravine we descended into the clouds yet came upon signs of life and growth – a huge beetle, bilberries, heather and mosses. Distantly, there were occasional glimpses of the A87. The drone of a passing car was at once comforting but, in that mountain fog, somewhat eerie. On the skyline way above and around us, the jagged outlines of the western subsidiaries of Fhuaran and Carnach were often visible. Their stark clarity contrasted sharply with the drifting belt of cloud through which we were scrambling. The going was horrible now: boulder scree, huge lumps of rock, because the ravine was the confluence of several very steep, very high screes. Mistily, there loomed up in front what looked like a garden shed but turned out to be a single boulder. Another of the same size blocked the gully and forced us to make a detour onto the scree slope itself. The rocky terrain was difficult, irksome, strenuous. Much of it was loose and slippery. So we skidded, stumbled and started little rock slides. But the vapourish greyness was thinning. Far below us were trees and green fields, toy-like cars moving lazily along Glen Shiel, and, beyond the road, a white cottage. Could we reach all that? Doubts were nourished by the height at which we were still poised. The glen was not far away, but our ravine obviously dropped suddenly – and that drop could not be far ahead.

Out of those wild rocks burst a sparkling little burn, dancing over and round the boulders and creating inviting little pools. Soda dived in, cooling the inner and outer dog, and then tried to find some kind of perch on those nasty rocks while I squatted to refill the water-bottle. But that laughing burn soon lost its charm. It became a dashing, crashing torrent tumbling down a great fall that was simply unclimbable. You see what I mean about the hazards of following a mountain stream? We had gone too far. Again we had to retreat – back up that devilish gully – and somehow find a way out. There were three possibilities. One, we would somehow scramble steeply up to the ravine's southern rim and thus gain easier ground for the descent. Two, we would have to go all the way back to the ridge and regain our earlier route. Three, we would have to spend the night on the mountain. The second possibility was unpleasant, the third unthinkable.

True, a night out would have been tolerable if uncomfortable. I had emergency rations, a survival bag, and plenty of warm clothing. In case of need I also had a torch and whistle with which to summon aid (on such a mass of broken rock one is conscious of the risk of twisting an ankle). The international distress signal is 6 blasts on the whistle – or flashes of the torch – at 10 second intervals for 1 minute, followed by a minute's pause before the process is repeated. The response is 3 blasts or flashes at 20 second intervals for 1 minute, followed by a similar minute's pause before the signal is repeated. But I was taking great care with my footwork. As for staying out for the night, that would have been acutely embarrassing because it could have led to a rescue operation. The ravine had no telephone box. There was no way of letting my hosts know that I would not be back until breakfast.

178

All this passed through the mind very quickly. The conclusion was inescapable: we must get down. The sides of that ravine were awfully steep but somehow there had to be a means of ascent that would be within Soda's capacities. There was nothing that obviously met such a requirement. But as we wandered back up that damnable gorge I saw a formidably abrupt bank of rock and heather that, faute de mieux, would have to do. While testing the strength of the heather and scanning the bank for any obtrusive rocks that might serve as footholds, I explained the situation to Soda. He did not want to know. He looked at me and he looked at that wall of heather, which, if not straight over his head, was as close to the vertical as made little difference. For the first time that day – or any other, for that matter – I had to coax and insist in turn. Then he went for it. I hauled him by the collar with one hand while hanging on with the other and hoping that neither of us would reel backwards. The worst was soon over. The angle of ascent soon became more accommodating and we scrambled over the top onto an open hillside west of Carnach. What a delightful sight it was after that horrid, claustrophobic ravine.

Richly clothed in vegetation, the slopes dropped sharply to Glen Shiel via a few craggy outcrops that were easily circumvented (we had spent enough time on rocks for one day). Thin clouds were drifting lazily across the tops, just as they had done that morning. The Sisters were still magnificently reserved, still irresistibly challenging. And had we stayed on course, the conventional descent down Coire na Criche, or from the western spur of Saighead, would have spared us all that nonsense in the gorge.

We followed a track alongside the River Shiel to the farm at Achnangart and had a last trek up the road to the car, passing that 1719 battleground on the way. The light was fading from the day and ghosts were roaming the glen. That brave Gordon Setter, all the bounce taken out of him, was padding along beside me like a shadow. We had covered about 12 map miles and it had taken us more

179

than 8 hours, plus almost 2 hours devoted to rest and refreshment. Driving back down Glen Shiel, I stopped beside the white cottage we had glimpsed in the distance while imprisoned among rocks (the inmates of Alcatraz must have felt much the same when looking across the bay to San Francisco). From a safe distance I stared back through the dusk at that deep, dark cleft in the mountain and realised that, while wanting to forget, I would always remember. Some word reflecting on its parentage may have slipped out.

Back at Kintail Lodge, I needed nothing more than a hot bath, a large fruit salad with cream, and vast quantities of beer. Before turning in, we had a last stroll by the softly lapping waters of Loch Duich and I reflected that, although the Five Sisters could be unreservedly recommended, there would be a cautionary tale to tell about the day Soda and his handler went to meet them. That night, we slept well.

Other suggested walks

1 The traverse of the Five Sisters can be abbreviated by descending steeply from the western spur of Sgurr Fhuaran.
2 The route for the South Glen Shiel Ridge starts from the Cluanie Inn, climbing to Creag a' Mhaim and following the ridge westward before descending from Creag nan Damh to the A87. There are alternative, earlier routes back down to Glen Shiel.
3 North-east of these walks is another, approached from Cannich, that is a fine sample of the area – taking in Loch Beinn a' Mheadhoin (starting point), Gleann nam Fiadh, Toll Creagach, Tom a' Choinich, Carn Eige, Mam Sodhail, and Sgurr na Lapaich back to Glen Affric.

12

Bikinis on Canisp

Assynt, in Sutherland, is a harshly surrealistic land. The sight of it challenges belief. The terrain is uneasily poised between truth and lies, between known quantities and the wanderings of a disordered mind. Its awful, slightly eerie, but fascinating grandeur is most easily appreciated via the straightforward ascent of Canisp, which is higher than anything else in the immediate neighbourhood except Cul Mor (and the difference is only 7ft). Canisp and Suilven, 2½ miles to the west, are isolated geological oddities. Such masses of Torridonian sandstone, embellished by the greys of quartzite, were once commonplace in Assynt. But most of them were gradually eroded and vanished from the landscape, which was thus reduced to its hard and level base of Lewisian gneiss. This supports a multitude of lochs and lochans that, visually, left this wild country in a weird half-world, a compromise between land and sea. As scenery goes, it would be too bleak to detain us long but for the fact that Canisp and Suilven (plus supporting cast) somehow survived the erosion. Deprived of such conventional adjuncts as foothills, they have an effect akin to that of great ships washed up on an otherwise empty beach. Imagine what the Houses of Parliament and Westminster Abbey would look like if the rest of London was razed to the ground, or Notre Dame and the Louvre if the same thing happened to Paris.

Sutherland, the 'Southland' of the Vikings, has little in common with the geographic norms of mainland Europe. In many ways it has a closer affinity with Scandinavia, Iceland and Greenland. This was the last chunk of Britain to break free from the ancient coating of ice, the last refuge for flora and wild-life more commonly associated

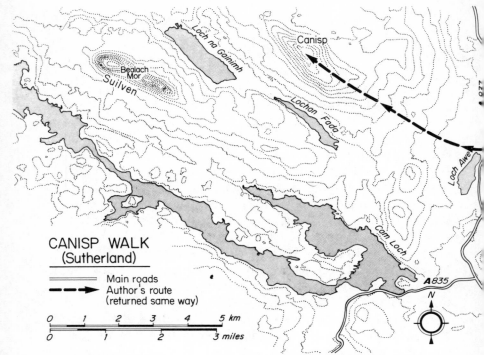

CANISP WALK
(Sutherland)

═══════ Main roads
▰▰▰▶ Author's route
(returned same way)

with the Arctic. It is a desolate, hostile wilderness that –
because of the mountains rising so abruptly from what is
almost an inland sea – has a unique, breathtaking
beauty. Another unique feature is that Sutherland lays
bare the history of geology and therefore, for much of the
year, has a transient population of students. Its rocks are
the oldest in Britain. They go back about 2,600 million
years, which means that they were formed before there
was life on Earth. The most evident rock is gneiss (from
an old German word for 'sparkle'), a metamorphosed
granite composed of laminated crystals of quartz, feldspar
and mica. This impervious gneiss explains the lochs and
lochans and serves as a foundation for the mountains.

The barren waste of rock and water makes it hard to
believe that, on and around an imaginary line from Loch
Assynt to the Point of Stoèr, there were prehistoric
settlements and, much later, summer shielings –
temporary shelters for cowherds. These shielings (a 'shiel'

or 'bothy' is a hut) often had turf walls with an inner lining of stone. Outside were pens for the livestock. The overgrown ruins are still there, in some unlikely places. The shielings mostly died during the clearances of the eighteenth and nineteenth centuries, when such farming settlements were evacuated to make way for sheep and later, in many areas, deer preserves. But a few survived to become permanent farms.

It is the eccentric landscape, though, that makes Sutherland such a strange, magical place. Scotland as a whole, of course, is somewhat embarrassing. The challenges are so abundant and diverse that the country might have been custom-built for those who walk in high places. A week in Scotland could offer rewarding days almost anywhere from Ben Lomond and The Cobbler all the way north past Ben Nevis and on to Foinaven (not far short of Cape Wrath), or across to the Cairngorms or, in the opposite direction, to the Cuillin Hills of Skye and other inviting protuberances on the Inner Hebrides. I chose three widely scattered areas with distinctive characters – the Ochils for a loosener on the hills, the Five Sisters of Kintail for a ridge walk, and Sutherland for a remote peak. The ultimate preference in Sutherland depended partly on where I could find a bed – plus such factors as the weather, explicit local information, an assessment of what would be safe for Soda, and the whim of the moment. The initial target, if only to establish that such a place was fact rather than fiction, was Inchnadamph.

At least the name made sense. 'Inch' (or 'eilean') refers to an island, 'uamh' to a cave, and 'na' and its variants means 'the', 'of', or 'of the'. We have already dipped briefly into the semantics peculiar to Scotland. It may be useful to do so again but we will keep the list short: 'ben' or 'beinn' (mountain), 'buachaille' (shepherd), 'cnoc' (hill), 'druim' or 'drum' (ridge), 'dubh' (dark), 'glas' (green), 'inver' (confluence or estuary), 'lairig' (pass), 'meall' (rounded hill), 'mor' (large), and 'stac' (steep rock or conical peak). That makes the map a little more intelligible. The most interesting feature of the map, though, is the way land and water dispute possession of the area between Inchnadamph and the Point of Stoer. This seems to be a part of the world that nature has left in the pending tray.

Unless you have a perverse fondness for midges, August is not the ideal month for Scottish exploration. Better to go between April and June, or in the autumn. But I was in no mood to cavil as we drove north on the loveliest of summer days and came within sight of Ullapool, which might be described as Britain's last resort. This smart and busy little port eagerly caters for the kind of tourists who consider the Ross and Cromarty of the shipping forecasts a remote and romantic location for holidays. Ullapool has a spectacular setting between the hills and the sea, and a row of white houses reaches out like an arm towards the fishing boats scattered about Loch Broom. The prettiness of Ullapool's immediate environment soon gave way to a bare landscape of mountains, lochs, lonely valleys and grassy knolls speckled with cream-coloured rocks. We passed through Elphin without really noticing that it was there. The views were clear and distant: the bulk of Canisp and, peeping out now and then, Suilven, one of those mountains that beg to be climbed. Just past Canisp, at the south-eastern extremity of Loch Assynt, I took the last available room at the Inchnadamph Hotel. Room 30 turned out to be uncomfortably hot (something to do with the kitchen below) but in every other respect the accommodation, like the weather, was perfect.

Basically for anglers, the hotel is also popular with walkers, climbers and geological students. What struck me at dinner that evening was the diversity of customers: wearing everything from suits and ties to shorts and sports shirts. In dining room and lounge in turn, we soon became a congenially easy-going little community in which, without prying, everyone took an interest in what the others were up to. The landlord, Willie Morrison, had his snug and roomy empire so well organised that all the right things seemed to happen naturally. The dining room was subject to the majestic authority of his daughter Annella, a bustling beauty who sailed round the tables like some proud galleon circumnavigating shoals. Untethered doilies fluttered in her wake. She knew what was happening everywhere, because she was making it happen.

That evening I emptied a few glasses in the company of her brother George and Jimmy and June Mackie. George and Jimmy, a deerstalker, are members of the Assynt mountain rescue team, for whom the Inchnadamph Hotel serves as a base, and June has done her stint on the telephone and radio ('I've seen me over here at two in the morning making sandwiches'). There can be no rest for the wives, anyway, until the men of the mountain rescue service are safely home. The Assynt team, formed in the middle 1970s by half a dozen shepherds and policemen, has become a large and well-organised service with twenty-four 'full' members, three probationers and fourteen reserves. Seven boats are available, because the loch is often the quickest way to an emergency, and they can also call on dogs from SARDA (the Search and Rescue Dogs Association), and RAF helicopters. The Assynt team cover a huge area bounded roughly by Cape Wrath and Strathy Point in the north, Dornoch in the south-east, and Lochinver in the west.

The call-out list is in the care of a policeman's wife at Lochinver. The team assembled depends partly on who happens to be available and partly on the nature of the incident – a general search, a climbing accident, or whatever. The work is entirely voluntary. 'We do it,' said Jimmy, 'because it's a job that has to be done.' What is annoying is that such rescue teams are inconvenienced – and even imperilled – far more often than they should be. 'We get a lot of false alarms and confusion,' said George. So that you and I might help to spread the word, I asked them to list some of the daft or merely imprudent things people did when roaming about such places as Assynt. Boiled down, the answers amounted to five points:

1 Too many people go out alone (two or more is safer) without telling anyone where they are going and what time they expect to be back. Rescue teams have been activated simply because somebody has gone fishing for the weekend, leaving a car by the roadside for two days or more without sticking a note on the windscreen or otherwise leaving details of their intentions.

2 Hill-walkers can get into trouble by failing to pack map and compass – or by using them incompetently. And rescue operations are much more complicated if the rescuees cannot indicate their whereabouts because they have forgotten to pack a torch (essential at night) or a whistle (essential in mist) with which to make the distress signals detailed in the previous chapter. Survival bags should be brightly coloured.

3 Unlikely though it seems, some visitors go scrambling, even climbing, in such flimsy footwear as sandshoes or sandals, or in high heels.

4 Just because it happens to be sunny and warm in the valleys, a naive or careless minority neglect to pack the windproof and waterproof clothing that they will probably need in the lower temperatures and more fickle weather over 2,000ft (610m).

5 Getting tired and cold can be particularly dangerous on the hills if one has no food in reserve. 'I always have one sandwich left in my pocket,' said Jimmy. 'Chocolate is a good thing to carry,' June added, 'because it raises the blood sugar.' Dehydration can also be a problem. Water must be carried, as there is seldom much of it about on the tops.

George suggested that basic first aid should be part of the school curriculum. 'So many simple things can save lives.' He also pointed out that communications were a big problem in the hills and that any form of radio communication could be useful. Like the mountain rescue service as a whole, the Assynt team are grateful to all kinds of people for the equipment necessary to their labours – radios, ropes, helmets, clothing, rucksacks, a Land Rover, petrol, and so on. Some of these items are donated. Others have to be bought; and the money comes from such local fund-raising schemes as raffles, sales of work, and slide shows. Mountain rescue is expensive – in addition to its human cost in terms of the time and effort put in by hardy volunteers who sometimes have to risk their own lives in trying to save others. So let us make sure, you and I, that all the common sense June and Jimmy and George were talking is more widely appreciated among the hill-walking fraternity, especially the young. The mountain rescue service and the dogs and handlers of SARDA (which is also a voluntary organisation) would have less to do if the public at large had a greater awareness of the causes, and effects, of a rescue operation.

Even more dog-conscious than usual, I decided to make do with Canisp (2,779ft or 847m). This could easily be linked with Suilven (2,399ft or 731m), via the path from Lochan Fada to Loch na Gainimh, but Suilven's reputation suggested that it was no place for Soda. For similar reasons Ben More Assynt (3,272ft or 997m) and Quinag (2,653ft or 809m) were also ruled out. Cul Mor (2,786ft or 849m) was no more inviting than the handier Canisp, and the unique, serrated crest of Stac Pollaidh (2,009ft or 612m) should come into view – from Canisp – without the bother of driving all the way to Loch Lurgainn. Next morning I telephoned the keeper, as Jimmy Mackie had suggested, to ensure that our modest ascent would not coincide with stalking. The keeper put my mind at ease on that score but asked me to keep the dog on a lead. There was a pause. I was not going to lie to him and he knew very well that no man was going to walk to the top of a mountain and back with a dog on a lead all the way. The keeper's alternative request, that the dog should be kept under close control, was more practicable. One has to be discreet and watchful when unleashing a dog on the hills, but discretion does not insist that dog and handler should be permanently attached.

Shooting and stalking parties are the chief source of income for many Highland estates. 'It's our job – we have to get our quota,' Jimmy told me. 'And it keeps a roof over our heads,' June added. 'Landowners – we call them lairds – employ a lot of people and provide housing.' From mid-July until the end of October hill-walkers should therefore find out whether stalking will be in progress over their planned route. For one thing, there may be bullets flying about. For another, a day's sport can be spoiled if a walker in brightly coloured clothing gets in the way and disturbs the game. On this question of colours Jimmy's working priorities conflict with his mountain rescue preferences. He knows that vivid colours frighten deer, grouse and other game. Equally, he knows that a lost or damaged hill-walker will, if wearing something gaudy, be easier to find. The compromise is to dress in dull colours but carry something more exciting in the rucksack – the survival bag and perhaps a spare sweater of the kind that shouts rather than whispers. It used to be the done thing to wear subdued colours on the hills, thus merging with the landscape and introducing no jarring notes into the scenery for anyone else who might happen to be around. A more personal benefit is that such camouflage gives one a much better chance to enjoy wild-life close at hand, rather than frightening it away. All that still makes sense. But nowadays there are hill-walkers who look like illuminated Christmas trees.

Predictably, the Inchnadamph Hotel did a good breakfast. Outside the dining room, packed lunches and flasks of coffee or tea were neatly arranged on several trays. I also had about a litre of fresh water for Soda. This was clearly going to be a day of glaring, oppressive heat, and the map and Jimmy had both reminded me that there were no burns on the heights of Canisp. I left a note of my intentions, the car's registration number, the colour of clothes and rucksack, and the fact that I was carrying a torch and a whistle. These written details seemed an excessive precaution for anyone setting out for a straightforward walk on a glorious day, but one must not break good habits. Accidents can happen. And the weather can change suddenly.

I parked near the northern end of Loch Awe and made for Canisp via a wooden footbridge and a bog that was crisp and springy after a recent dry spell. Then we were up among rocks and heather, taking a rough line from the cairns. Soda, into every pool, once vanished from sight for a moment and then came up for air, looking startled. He also had a little trouble dragging himself out of some boggy water. I was watching him, but letting him learn sense the hard way. Stopping briefly for elevenses, I looked down on Loch Awe and its smaller neighbours and, unexpectedly, an aircraft (perhaps from Lossiemouth) roaring down the valley of the River Loanan. To see an aircraft hurtling by, far below, is rather startling confirmation that one is gaining height. The view of mountains and lochs was expanding. Close at hand, the rocks were a visually pleasing light grey but, in that heat, the ascent had become a tough plod. Soda twice looked at me oddly, as if to say 'What happened to the downhill part of my life?'. Then we were over the shoulder of Canisp and had grassy, springy going all the way to the top.

Canisp is not a particularly striking mountain, though its bulk is impressive and its height respectable. There are two odd features. Imagine, if you will, that an unusually long mountain has been cut in half and one half removed. The other strange thing about Canisp is that the remaining half rises steadily from the bog at an angle much like that of a children's slide. Consequently one labours up a long, sloping ridge (the width of a couple of motorways) that seems to go on for ever, always rising, until it ends abruptly on the edge of emptiness. Again, just like a children's slide. At the top there is nothing but space, a vertiginous drop, and a breathtaking, improbably dramatic panorama. This 'big finish' is all the more astonishing because the humdrum ascent gives us not the slightest hint that Canisp is suddenly going to stop in mid-air.

On the summit there are two rough stone shelters. On such a day these were redundant. But just beyond one of them was a spot that gave us some protection from the fierce heat and the inevitable wind. Tucked among the rocks over that plunging, amazing view, I measured out Soda's water ration and we then took lunch. Thank goodness he was too tired to gad about, dancing on air. He looked out on that shimmering immensity of lochs and lochans and intervening mountains, a totally alien world. Then he settled down for a nap, putting a forepaw on one of my boots in such a relaxed way that it seemed accidental. But it was nothing of the sort. He needed the reassurance of something familiar. By now, I knew the routine. We stayed there for an hour and a quarter. I had nothing better to do and, having neglected to bring a camera, wanted to etch on my mind for ever the extraordinary beauty of that golden prospect from the summit of Canisp. So I sat and looked and dreamed – and cherished one of those sublime assaults on the senses that, on rare occasions, extravagantly reward us for the sweat of climbing mountains.

From that rocky platform in the sky we looked out to the Western Isles and the Atlantic and, all around, the lochs and the Highlands. Loch Assynt stretched out lazily in the mid-day heat. Stac Pollaidh etched playful doodles into the south-western skyline. But Suilven, topographically in the same family, was the most arresting spectacle of them all. For their size, Stac Pollaidh and Suilven may be the most bizarre and fascinating mountains in Britain. In their shapes and settings they are far more extra-

(*above*) Loch Duich and the Five Sisters of Kintail (*Scottish Tourist Board*)
(*below*) Canisp from Cam Loch, Sutherland (*W. A. Poucher*)

(*above*) The bizarre and fascinating Suilven (*Ken Andrew*); (*below*) Suilven,
Canisp and the desolate Sutherland terrain (*Scottish Tourist Board*)

ordinary than, for example, Tryfan. From east or west,
Suilven looks conical. In fact the mountain is a mile and a
half long and has three peaks. It manages to be
simultaneously impressive and amusing – the latter
because Suilven has a hint of affectation about it, as if too
self-consciously mountainous. That craggy giant has such
a strong personality that one inevitably writes about it in
human terms. If you asked a child to make a plasticine
model incorporating his or her preconceptions about
mountains, the result would probably be a shorter form of
Suilven. Even Loch na Gainimh, which fills the hollow
between Canisp and Suilven, is so neatly arranged that it
could be part of some human rather than natural design.
Musing on all this, I turned to look again at distant Stac
Pollaidh. Then the wandering peaks of Quinag, beyond
Loch Assynt. And all the other hills and mountains,
which rose so sharply from the watery wilderness that
they were like islands left high and dry by a tide that had
long since ebbed.

That marvellous spectacle could have filled the
afternoon. But Soda was getting restlessly explorative,
so it seemed prudent to retreat from the brink. Going
down, we disturbed some ptarmigan. These are chiefly
associated with the arctic tundra but turn up occasionally
on the heights of Sutherland. We passed within a couple
of yards of them but, had they not moved, might have
been unaware of their presence. The grey summer
plumage was a perfect camouflage amid the rocks. I came
across an enormous caterpillar, too. Scattered flora,
handfuls of beauty in an environment of desolate
grandeur, sprouted from little pockets of soil. Four slowly
moving figures on the way up gradually became
identifiable as two couples. One of the men told me they
had viewed Canisp from Suilven the day before and were
now in the course of doing the opposite. I envied them
Suilven, I said, but it hardly seemed the place to take a
dog. He grinned. 'No hope. I had misgivings about my
wife, never mind a dog.' In retrospect, though, I was

lazy. On such a perfect day one should have started a little earlier, climbed Canisp, returned to its lower slopes, traversed across to Bealach Mor on Suilven, and sampled as much of that splendid mountain as was safe for Soda. Instead, we were making a day out of what was no more than an afternoon's walk.

The two ladies wore the hill-walker's conventional boots and socks but nothing else except bikinis. No doubt they had something more substantial in the rucksacks. As it was, their imaginative application of the 'mix and match' system was perfectly adapted to the terrain and the heat. Irrelevant though it may be, they were easy on the eye because they had the kind of figures that justify exposure. More to the point, they looked comfortable and as cool as anyone could reasonably hope to be on such a sweltering day. A lot of nonsense is talked and written about the wrappings appropriate to hill-walking. Beware the temptation of fancy clothing at fancy prices. We need to invest in boots and thick socks, possibly a pair of breeches, and (unless we have one already) a parka that is windproof and waterproof. Other than all that, the older, neglected contents of drawers and wardrobes can be given another airing. They serve our purpose. The rest is vanity.

Boots are the most important item. Ordinary shoes can be dangerously slippery on grass and rock and tend to get torn to shreds anyway. Stoutly made shoes with formal uppers but commando-type soles are useful for casual outings. They are heavier than most shoes but worth the weight because of their two functions. For genuine hill-walking, boots are stronger, more comfortable, give the ankles some support, and are more effective in keeping the feet dry and free of grit and vegetation. They are made for the job, with sewn-in tongues and padding round the ankles. Moreover, boots need cost no more than a good pair of shoes. We must be sure they fit perfectly, because an ill-fitting pair waste money and ensure suffering (chafing, blisters, blackened toe-nails, and so on). Boots need to be at least one size larger than everyday shoes. Wear two pairs of thick socks when you try them on. Without flopping about, the boots should allow some freedom for wiggling the toes. If in doubt, try another pair. Take your time. In the cause of comfort, efficiency and a long life, one's boots demand continual care. After use, wash off the muck. When the boots are almost dry but still slightly damp, rub in one of those special waxes. Use your fingers, because the warmth and softness help. Pay particular attention to welts and seams. Then store the boots under cover but not near a radiator.

There are differing opinions about how far one should go to prevent water and more irritating junk from finding a way down into the boots. Gaiters, covering the calves and part of the boots, are effective and have become popular, but can be fussy and sweaty. The shorter, outer pair of socks (the inner pair are tucked into the breeches) do the job well enough if rolled loosely over the boot-tops. As for the socks, some people like a thin pair underneath but I prefer both pairs thick, with plenty of wool in them. These have a cushioning effect and provide warmth and insulation, too. Wool, warmth and insulation are important. Wet or dry, wool is a good insulator. Warmth is essential because a serious drop in body heat can lead to the dangerous form of exhaustion recognised by tiredness, coldness and loss of appetite (at a time when one needs food, especially sweet food, most urgently). The extremities – feet, hands and head – lose heat fastest. For normal hill-walking I prefer fingerless gloves to the warmer mittens, because there is no need to take them off when fiddling with the rucksack or the compass. Half the time, my hands are in my pockets anyway. As for the head, indulge your fancy – as long as the chosen headgear is warm and will not vanish from sight in a strong wind. Remember that the hood on your parka is not there simply for decoration.

Insulation is a question of retaining body heat by sealing it, more or less. We need some wool around us but insulation is achieved by the number of layers, not their thickness. Outer clothing, part of the insulation, should be windproof – and waterproof, too, unless waterproofs are carried separately in the rucksack. Go for zips rather than buttons, because zips are more weatherproof and, when one's fingers are cold, easier to open and close. Above all, we have to remember that although the bikini type of exposure is all very well, the other type can kill. Most such deaths arise from being weary and wet and cold. Paradox though it may seem, food – even if we have no appetite for it – is the first remedy to seek. And it works fast.

Soda's problem, as we came down from Canisp that afternoon, was that he needed a drink. His water supply had been exhausted and we had a long, hot plod over mostly stony ground before descending to burn-level. He panted patiently along until we came to a pool. It was perfectly designed for his needs, exactly the right depth, and he simply walked into the middle of it and ambled around, ducking his head to take in great gulps. He had his fun, cooled off inside and out, and then we clumped back across the bog to the car. Not counting breaks, we had spent almost 4 hours dawdling over about 8 easy miles. But the fierce heat was some excuse for loitering. And presumably we had established some totally irrelevant record by coming across ptarmigan and bikinis on the same mountain the same afternoon. There were some strange birds on Canisp that day.

Back at the hotel, returning guests were sunshine-pink. Those of us who had been on the mountains had the kind of thirsts better quenched via buckets rather than glasses. I collected a pint and walked out to the foyer to telephone my wife. But a startling apparition appeared at the hotel door. He was wearing shirt, shorts, boots, and rucksack and was heavily coated in dried sweat. He was also panting, audibly. Two staring eyes focussed on my pint. Thus must Leander and Hero have looked when they drowned in the same sea. In a foreign accent he found the

breath for three words: 'Vare ist bar?' I had seen eyes like
that before, on men prepared to kill. The lad's need was
desperate. I offered him my pint and he drained half of it
as if taking in air. He recovered, though, and kept us
awake half the night playing a mouth-organ.

There was plenty of time before dinner, but an
overwhelming lassitude prevented me from exploring the
vicinity of Inchnadamph more thoroughly. It has caves, a
nature reserve, and, just up the road by Loch Assynt, the
ruins of Calda House and Ardvreck Castle. Calda House,
known locally as 'White House', was built in 1660 for the
Earl of Seaforth. The sad remnants of Ardvreck Castle,
on a rocky peninsula, have a more prominent place in
Scottish history. Built in the sixteenth century, Ardvreck
was the seat of the powerful Macleods of Assynt – and the
place where the romantic career of James Graham,
Marquess of Montrose (1612–50), came to an end. This
remarkable man, a soldier and lyric poet, was an
inspiring and successful general who did much for the
royalist cause before Charles I lost his head in 1649. Then
Cromwell moved in – and Montrose became a rebel. In
1650 Montrose lost the Battle of Carbisdale (by the Kyle
of Sutherland) and fled to Assynt. There are two stories
about what happened next, and the truth cannot be
established. One story is that Macleod found Montrose
on the moors, arrested him, and handed him over to
higher authorities. The other is that Montrose, exhausted,
sought refuge at Ardvreck, where Macleod was initially a
kind host but then betrayed Montrose because of the price
on his head. Either way, Montrose was held at Ardvreck
before being hanged in Edinburgh.

All that, plus Suilven and the Inchnadamph Hotel,
would more than justify another trip to Assynt, I decided.
Meantime I had dinner. When the fair Annella saw me
retreating upstairs with the remnants of the main course,
she called me back and topped up Soda's bonus with a
few goodies from the joint. Later I brought him down to
the lounge, and other guests (they knew where we had

197

been) came across and enquired how that tired, sleeping Gordon Setter had coped with Canisp in such enervating heat. One lady told me, in the softest of Scottish accents, that she and her husband had spent the day fishing. She had kept looking up at that sun-hot mountain, she said, wondering if she might spot us, and sighing 'That puer wee dog'. Soda did rather well for sympathy that evening.

Next morning, driving south, I stopped briefly at Elphin for a last look across the intervening lochs and hills towards the grotesque Suilven and the vast bulk of Canisp. Scotland had been kind to us. We had sampled its heights in three small but undiluted nips. Canisp, where this book ends, had been even sunnier than Dartmoor, where it began. By accident rather than design, Soda and I had even bagged three Munros, not counting the retreat from Sgurr Fhuaran. Just 273 to go. See you on the tops.

Other suggested walks

1 In addition to the Canisp–Suilven route mentioned in this chapter, Suilven can be tackled directly from the A835 via Cam Loch and Lochan Fada, with possible extensions from Suilven to Glencanisp Lodge and Lochinver, or to the Falls of Kirkaig and Inverkirkaig.
2 A short circuit of Stac Pollaidh can be made from a parking area by Loch Lurgainn.
3 Quinag is best approached from Skiag Bridge (Loch Assynt). The route is via Spidean Coinich to Sail Gharbh and possibly Sail Gorm before descending to Lochan Bealach Cornaidh.

Appendix: The Rucksack

The rucksack is the hill-walker's wardrobe, kitchen and general storage unit. It must therefore be chosen and packed with care. Those who intend to bivouac, with or without mountaineering equipment, or to go on tour without a car, need the larger type of framed rucksack. The frame prevents the rucksack from rubbing on the back and also permits air to get between rucksack and back, thus discouraging sweat. A frameless rucksack must be packed so that nothing hard sticks in the back. The average hill-walker, who just goes out for the day, can make do with a smaller, lighter rucksack. My own weighs only 26oz (740g) and is probably the smallest available 'day sack' with a frame (in this case, a frame of the most basic kind). If we can find a large plastic bag to serve as an inner lining, that will keep everything dry. Alternatively, selected individual items can be kept dry in plastic bags of more readily available sizes. Weight can most easily be carried in the area of the shoulders, at the top of the spine. The rucksack's lighter contents should therefore be packed at the bottom. We need a balanced load with its main weight at the top.

For the benefit of newcomers to the hills and those whose know-how has for some reason rusted, my personal check-list (kept in the flap pocket of the rucksack at all times) is reproduced below with a few explanatory notes. It includes everything – except a shirt, which none of us is likely to forget – that I will probably want to wear or carry. Inevitably there will be variations according with personal preferences, the weather, and so on. But this list is, I hope, a reliable fundamental guide that you can adjust at will.

Clothing

Boots; socks (long and short); breeches; thermal under-wear; sweaters (one thick and one or two thin); parka; over-trousers; Balaclava; fingerless gloves. *Note* I have friends who carry an extra windproof and/or waterproof jacket.

Food and drink

Fruit; sultanas or raisins; dates; chocolate; boiled sweets; mint cake; fruit cake; sandwiches; water; hot soup or coffee; wine; tin-opener; knife. *Note* This list includes both day-time snacks and emergency rations, to be kept in reserve. All is nutritional, most of it light (except for the liquids), and much of it sweet. The fruit usually consists of two or three oranges. I eat well at breakfast and at evening dinner and find that, during the day, I need refuelling only in small quantities.

Safety

Map; compass; torch; whistle; survival bag. *Note* The torch can also be useful for map-reading at dusk. Plastic survival bags and mountain distress whistles are available at most specialist shops.

Miscellaneous

Garbage bag; spare bootlaces; plasters and/or first-aid kit; toilet paper; pipe, tobacco, matches or lighter; wallet; camera; tape recorder; notebook and pencil; dog food, dish and lead. *Note* Several of these items are obviously optional. For the dog I also take a towel, brush and bedcover, but leave these in the car or hotel.

That list looks long, but I never take the lot and nor will you. In any case, it is amazing how much can be accommodated in even a relatively small rucksack if one packs carefully.

Acknowledgements

As is evident in these pages I am greatly indebted to the friends, old and new, who so kindly gave me their encouragement, advice and companionship when and where the need arose. It is not necessary to name all of them here, because they have been named already, but special thanks are due to Keith Watson for his thoughtful diligence in ensuring that my wanderings in the northern Pennines and the Lake District would be adequately supervised.

Thanks to the sympathetic expertise of Gerald Style of Runfold, Roger Gould of Melbourne, and other professional advisers, my photographs are far better than they might have been. Finally, beaucoup de remerciements to Keith Dickson of Agence France Presse, who loaned me his typewriter for a fortnight (my own had jammed) and thus enabled me to write Chapters 6 and 7 in a Paris hotel room.

Bibliography

Of the many books and leaflets consulted, the following were probably the most useful.

Gemmell, Arthur, *Three Peaks Footpath Map and Guide*, Stile Pubns (1980)

Hay, David and Joan, *Mardale, The Drowned Village*, Friends of the Lake District (1976)

Millward, Roy and Robinson, Adrian, *Upland Britain*, David & Charles (1980)

Sharp, David, *Walking in the Countryside*, David & Charles (1978)

Smith, Roger (ed), *Walking in Scotland*, Spurbooks (1981)

Watson, Keith, *Walking in Teesdale*, Dalesman Books (1978)

Wilson, Ken and Gilbert, Richard, *The Big Walks*, Diadem Books (1980)

—— *Classic Walks*, Diadem Books (1982)

Yorkshire's Three Peaks, Dalesman Books (1978)

Dictionary of National Biography, OUP

Index

203

205